Nobody Dies in Art Class

and Other Valuable Art Lessons That Will Inspire Your Life

Elida Field

ISBN: 979-8-9888779-0-5

Dedication

This book is dedicated to:
all my students both young and old who were willing to give art a chance and allow me to guide them in connecting to their creativity,

And:
Shirley Bjur, my mom, who by osmosis taught me almost everything I know about teaching. She is a legend in her field and has changed so many lives, not only in the classroom, but by her example and the way she lives her life.

Table of Contents

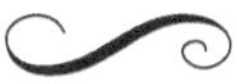

Acknowledgments

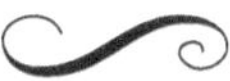

First, I would like to thank my sister, Danielle Harris, who is not only a brilliant writer herself but also an incredibly talented editor. She encouraged me to write this book and held my hand through the entire process. She has always been my best protector and biggest fan and I love her to the moon and back.

I would also like to acknowledge my kids who have been a big part of my journey and have helped me pursue my dreams. I would not be the woman I am today without first being their mother. In many ways, they have been my best teachers.

Lastly, I would like to acknowledge my soul sisters, students, friends, and family who have signed up to do this life with me. They have encouraged me and surrounded me with a safety net of love, allowing me to jump freely into almost any adventure I find. I know that they are there to catch me when I fall. I am beyond blessed and truly grateful.

Preface

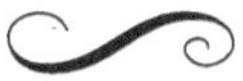

When you walk into my art studio, you think you are coming to learn how to paint. You would rarely guess, or even dare to hope, that painting could lift you out of a depression, comfort you after a devastating loss or a messy divorce, or even fill the vacant and listless hours of your empty nest with a new community of friends. No doubt, an art class can teach you how to "make art"—how to mix colors, how to soften a painting with a wash and tie it together, and how to walk away from a painting before you overdo it. But did you know that painting, or any creative process for that matter, is a training ground for life? The challenges you face and eventually overcome within art class can serve as the drills and exercises that will build you up and make you ready to face other difficult situations.

For twenty-some years, I have taught art to thousands of kids, teens, and adults, and it still amazes me when I get to witness the miraculous transformation that happens to individuals as they paint and create. There is the hyperactive boy, unable to sit still for more than a few minutes, who becomes quiet and enthralled for an hour- long art lesson. Or the insecure teen, hiding behind her hair, who blossoms into a strong, competent young adult because of her artistic endeavors. Or the brokenhearted woman, dragging herself out of bed to attend art class, who becomes a vibrant, thriving artist and leader, eventually empowering other women in their creative endeavors. There is even the man, representing a small and beloved percentage of my clientele, who discovers a breakthrough at his job from his time spent creating and painting. These are actual stories, and yet they represent many. Coming to my little painting class has been a pivotal event for many of my art students who claim: "I see the world differently now."

This book is an effort to share with you, the reader, the same inspiring lessons I give to my students. I hope that, as you read these stories, you will see yourself in them, and by the end of this book, you will find a way through whatever struggles you are facing—whether it's on the canvas, in your relationships, or deep within your own thinking or heart.

Note: This book reflects my present recollections of experiences over time. Some names and characteristics have been changed, some events have been compiled, and some dialogue has been recreated.

Chapter 1:

Your Art Isn't for Everyone

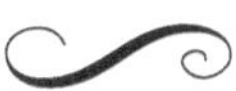

Meg pulled me aside right after Art-Women-Wine class to talk about her most recent Facebook crisis.

She whispered, "I'm about ready to pull my artwork off all social media!" Tears filled her eyes.

"What happened?" I asked.

"Do you know how you can pay for ads on Facebook to get more people to see your stuff?" I nodded.

"I was trying to hit my target audience," she continued. "Instead, I've gotten all these mean remarks from people. They are saying such hurtful things that I want to take down all my paintings and not show anyone. Ever." Now the tears were welling up. I could see the hurt on her face.

I asked to look over the Facebook ad and see which settings she had used. After reading through the comments and investigating the situation, it became apparent that maybe Facebook had spammed her account to people who weren't interested. This was an odd situation, and the reality wasn't necessarily that people didn't like her artwork but rather they were tired of Facebook deciding what they should see. I could relate to this problem, but their reactions were wrong, taking out their frustrations on Meg instead of Facebook. Several of the comments were "SPAM" and "Why the heck am I seeing this sh*t?"

"Meg," I said, "these people aren't *your* people. Facebook messed up. The algorithm just sent it out to everyone instead of people who might be interested in art like yours. It is not a reflection of who you are as an artist!" She nodded, still a little shaken and fragile. "Your work is beautiful. Think about that giraffe painting you just sold to the sweet couple on the East Coast. Remember the massive triptych that hangs in the local elementary school and how so many people comment on it? Your work is loved by many people. It's important. Valuable. But your art isn't for everyone and that's okay! Let's find the people that your artwork is for!" She exhaled a long sigh, and I reached around her shoulders to give her a soft squeeze. We chatted a little longer about her current art piece and upcoming ideas before parting ways to finish our day.

Part of being an artist is understanding that neither you nor your art will be liked by everyone. Some people will love your art, and some won't. There's just no getting around it. That's what makes art so wonderful—that there is something for everyone, *but you don't have to be everything for everyone.*

When I was younger, I was on a mission to make sure that I was liked by everyone. I had the audacity to believe that I had succeeded for years until I decided to volunteer as a coach for my daughter, Emily's volleyball team. I was an All-American setter in college and had coached at the collegiate level, so I felt confident to take on a group of middle schoolers. Most of the girls had never played volleyball before and my goal was to teach them the basics so they could make their school teams but also to build their confidence as young women.

By the end of the season, I had built an excellent rapport with the girls. Since my focus wasn't on wins but on growth and maturity, I had some unique rules. I wouldn't tolerate bad behavior. If a girl rolled her eyes at me or was rude to a teammate, she'd be taking a break on the bench, even if she was the best player on the team. I would rather lose a game (and that's saying a lot since I am ultracompetitive) than win with a disrespectful group of girls. It was the last tournament and we played well overall, but we ended up losing. Still, I felt proud of how far we had come, moving up through rankings from thirty-fifth to thirteenth—an impressive achievement for a group of girls who hadn't played before.

After our final team meeting and group hug, I was packing up my stuff when I saw two moms marching towards me. I felt a shift in energy. They looked angry. Unconsciously, I backed up toward the wall as they pressed in. I could feel their steaming breath on my face as they spit out insults and accusations. At first, I tried to explain but when that didn't pacify them, I blurted, "Even if we won first place, I think you'd still complain about me!"

The other mom shouted, "Well, if you had won, that would be the girls, but if you lose, that's on you!" I stayed quiet. Then, she yelled, "*I hate you!*" I stood there, shocked. As I looked past the mean moms, I saw my girls looking scared and sad. They must have felt conflicted seeing their moms, whom they loved, and me, whom they had grown to love, having such a visible and vicious argument. My heart broke. My face crumpled as I walked away in tears, completely devastated.

When I got home from the tournament, I physically got sick. It took me four days to get out of bed. As I stood at the counter, cooking breakfast, I had an epiphany. *Elida,* I thought to myself, *not everyone likes you! In fact, no matter how awesome you are, no matter what you do, they may still not like you! There are some people you just can't win over.*

The troll moms from volleyball will never like me and that's okay. I know that I gave everything I had to their daughters. When I learned that each girl I had trained made the volleyball team at their schools the next year, I breathed a sigh of satisfaction. My mission was accomplished.

Looking back, I find it humorous that it took me until my thirties to figure this out. I decided from that day on to focus on loving those who love me back. And move on from those who don't. I know that sounds selfish but there are so many people on this planet who love you, so focus on them. Spend your time with those who will appreciate you.

A few years later, after I had mastered my *Love those who love you* mantra, I was in New York City. Like a bright-eyed little girl on Christmas morning, I stepped into the Chelsea district of art lofts and galleries. I had my business cards in my purse and a truckload of enthusiasm to accomplish my dream of becoming represented at a New York City gallery. I walked through a tall glass door and saw a slew of paintings that looked familiar, like maybe I had seen them in art magazines or books. Brazenly and naively, I handed my card to the gallery director and said, "I'm not sure if you are accepting new artists, but, if you have a chance to look at my art, I think my work would be an amazing addition to your gallery."

An older woman looked down at me over her bifocals and said, "Most of our artists are dead!"

Without hesitation, I snapped back my card from her hand and retorted, "Well, I am very much alive, so this isn't the gallery for me. Toodle-loo!" And I sauntered out of the gallery. My younger self would have been shocked at the cold reception. I might have even argued that it was possible I could die at any time so investing in my artwork now might be a good idea. The older and wiser me, however, knew that this wasn't the gallery for me. It didn't matter how amazing my artwork was because these folks weren't my biggest fans. Even if I convinced them to take my work, they wouldn't sell it because they didn't believe in me.

In your quest as an artist—or really anything that you are pursuing—remember to pay attention to those who love you. Focus on the people who really believe in you and support you and let go of trying to make everyone your friend or convincing everyone to like you or your work.

But what do you do when you must go through rejection on a greater level? What do you do when the stakes are higher and it's not just a rejection of your artwork but a rejection of you?

Your art isn't for everyone.
Neither are you.

I had met him at college thirteen years prior. He was funny, adventurous, exciting and deep. He came from a good family and seemed to have everything I wanted in a potential mate. He made me laugh and I made him better. Within six months of meeting, we were married, and we were going to have a long and wonderful life together, or so I believed.

We had our daughter, Emily, and all was going well. Then I discovered a lie. Then a half-truth. A separate account. A message from another. How could it be? How could he reject me? I tried so hard to please him. Why wasn't it enough? And what would that mean for us? Emily was just three years old and now I was pregnant with our son. We all needed him.

But when I discovered another lie, I decided to separate. I moved back to Washington and moved in with my parents, a day before my 24th birthday and my dad's 50th. I remember leaving Texas, looking at everything I had worked for in building our little home and life together and realizing that I may never see it again. I ended up having Caleb, our second son, alone. Well, not exactly alone—my parents and cousins were there in the delivery room to cheer me on and Dad even cut the cord. But my husband wasn't there. I was so brokenhearted. For a year, we were apart. He continued living in Texas and I was trying to start over where I grew up in Washington. It was the hardest and longest year of my life. Eventually, however, he moved to be near the kids, and I decided to trust him again. I loved him. He was the father of our children. Perhaps my love could save us.

After getting back together, we had our third child, Weston. We built a beautiful home. We started a new business together. From the outside, it all looked like it was going so well. Yet, there were the arguments. When I had some time to myself, it seemed like the lows outnumbered the highs. It seemed like he was becoming more controlling, volatile, and isolating. If I was honest with myself, I was miserable and slowly dying inside. I couldn't understand why things were so bad when I was trying so hard, doing all of the right things.

When I found out about his continued infidelity, it all made sense. As awful as it was, it was a relief to know that all those feelings, the years of emptiness and questioning had an answer. I believed that all of that loving, and striving, and pleasing, and crying, and hoping was enough to heal him, heal us, and heal our marriage. But I was wrong. I realized that no matter how amazing or awesome I was, nothing would keep him from cheating. The tumbling down of our marriage and the tearing apart of our family was excruciating. The rejection was equally as painful.

That realization is hard because it means you have no control over the situation, only control over yourself and how you handle it. So here I was now without an answer or a plan. I couldn't fix him, and I couldn't fix this. I was stuck with that sick feeling and realization that this marriage was irreparable, but I needed to keep my head up for my kiddos. It was me, plus three, and an art degree. How was I going to make it?

Chapter 2:

Always Mix Your Colors

It was the first class for Art-Women-Wine and I handed out a sheet that read “Elida’s Fab Five.” Since my tech skills were lacking, the chart just had the different paints listed out with a simple plus sign between them and then an equal sign for the new color. The women stared at the paper, unenthused.

Mari raised her hand and half asked, half complained: “Why are we doing this? It’s going to take a lot more time and I already have these pre-mixed colors that I want to use.” She lifted one of her tubes of paint out of her art bag to show me. Other women murmured in agreement. I could sense a mutiny stirring.

It was time to share my story about Leslie. Leslie was my art instructor at college. I wasn't sure if Leslie was her first or last name and I knew better than to ask her. She wore an original eighties mullet, parted down the middle with feathered wings on the sides and long, straight, dishwater blond hair swinging down her back. It was the classic "business in the front and party in the back," and the style had stopped being cool over a decade ago. She wore Wranglers every day. And for Dallas, Texas, she defied convention because she wore no makeup.

Leslie transferred that same sense of comfort in who she was to her artwork and teaching. She didn't care about pleasing people—she'd tell you straight up if she thought your work was crap. She was an absolute zealot about mixing colors. She didn't like us to use what she called "cheater colors." Still, I would always hide a few tubes in my bag, just in case I couldn't mix the right one.

That is, until the incident with Jim. An accomplished artist, Jim's technique and perspective were always spot on. One day, he was showing us his latest masterpiece: a beautiful, high-contrast painting of Jesus on the cross. We were all gathered around admiring it when Leslie walked in. She strolled by in her easy, Texan kind of way, smacking some Juicy Fruit gum, and glanced over, noticing the painting before walking on.

Jim excitedly asked her, "Well, what do you think?"

She casually glanced in his direction. "Not bad, Jimmy. It's too bad you didn't bother to mix your black. Mars Black, right?" Jim's mouth dropped open and he started to stammer an argumentative reply, but Leslie had already moved on. We slowly dispersed to our seats. I slid down in my chair and stealthily moved my tube of Mars Black down toward the bottom of my bag so she wouldn't see it.

After that incident, I vowed to learn to mix my colors, like for real—no more cheater colors. Now, I consider mixing colors one of my superpowers. I can mix almost anything with just three colors, and with five colors, I have the flexibility to get any color I wish.

The women seemed to be a little more invested in mixing colors after that story, and so we began with Elida's Fab Five:

- Alizarin Crimson
- Phthalo Blue
- Ultramarine Blue

- Cadmium Red
- Cadmium Yellow

Add Titanium White, which isn't technically a color, so I call it a bonus, and I have everything I need to complete any painting.

The first lesson was to choose a magazine picture, cut out four or five holes from it, and glue it onto a sheet of white paper. Next, they had to mix their colors to fill in the holes in the magazine picture. The ladies all did a pretty good job except for Jennie who, in desperation, couldn't get the color to match a windowsill and decided to paint the whole magazine windowsill a new color that she made up! I had to give her kudos for creative problem-solving.

Eventually, after mixing to match their magazine picture, it was time to play. I encouraged everyone to mix their paints to make new colors. To make taupe, for instance, first mix black, brown, and add a little white. If it pulls too pink, add yellow which often saves the day. All this must be learned through practice, though.

I preach the Fab Five because I wholeheartedly believe in them. By exploring these basic guidelines, you gain enough confidence to create some amazing pieces. On the other hand, if you skip this step and just jump into painting without knowing how to mix, the opposite can happen: you will end up with a painting that looks canned, like a paint-by-numbers piece. Or the colors become muddy. I always start with how to paint with the Fab Five as a foundation for any painting I do. As you get better at painting, you can sprinkle in more colors, but you always have these five colors on your palette as a home base. And you use the mixing sheet like a Bible to guide you.

I was reminded of this lesson when I did a live painting for our church. For this piece, I decided to paint a giant world on a huge canvas and then paint Jesus on the cross over the top. I had about five minutes to paint it while the choir sang. I only brought a few colors because I was planning on being a minimalist; I wouldn't have enough time to fill the images with a lot of color in just five minutes. After I finished, I returned to my seat. But as the pastor walked onto the stage, he asked me if I would continue the painting as he preached. I happily agreed, but when I walked over to my palette, I realized I hadn't brought my Fab Five. In fact, I hadn't even brought one type of blue. No blue for the blue planet.

I began to sweat but it was too late. I was already on stage in front of hundreds of people, and I wanted to maintain professionalism. I wiped my forehead and then added red and a lot of gold. I tried to make it more of a monochromatic version of the world—in warm tones, of course—never letting on that I didn't bring blue. The piece still turned out well, but it was very stressful. I got a few questions afterwards from people: why did you decide to paint the world red and gold?

Like the true professional artist that I was, I quickly pivoted with, "You know, I was thinking about the blood of Jesus covering the whole world. The color crimson is so symbolic!" I pledged to never do that again.

If we look at the colors of Elida's Fab Five as the key friends or relationships in our lives, we can see how crucial it is to have the right ones to create that strong foundation. Evaluate the people you spend time with. You need at least three good friends, just like you need a minimum of three solid colors. Five is better, but with three, you can mix just about anything. You are the one who blends the experiences with your friends, deciding how much time to spend with them. If your closest friends aren't lifting you up, they may need to be treated like bonus colors, which are those colors that you add to your palette intermittently and in smaller doses.

List the people you spend time with and fill in the blanks to this statement for each of them: *"After I spend time with ________________, I always feel___________________________.*" Next to their names, write a number from one to ten that represents how you feel after you spend time with them—one being you'd rather stick a fork in your eye and ten being you feel like a rockstar! Circle the people who make you feel the best. If you didn't circle at least three friends, write a description of an imaginary friend. You can even give her a special name. Example: *My friend Awesome Annie is a creative writer. She calls me about twice a week and we get together for special dinners and lunches about two times a month. She always encourages me and gives me great insight into my business and family life. When I finish my time with Awesome Annie, I feel like a ten.* With these statements, you are writing down with intention the type of friends you are inviting into your life.

Next, on a new piece of paper, list the people who you circled. Next to their names assign a color. I've listed the descriptions below for each color. Remember, white is not a color, but it is always present. White represents God, that omniscient presence and guiding light in your life.

Red: passionate, strong, and bold. A little goes a long way, but a painting is dull without it. These people bring the fun factor! You need someone like this to remind you that life should be enjoyed. They bring out your wild side and ignite that fire burning within you. They are usually your biggest cheerleaders when you are about to embark on something new or take a leap of faith.

Yellow: bright, cheery, kind, and easy. This is probably the most common color in a painting. It is necessary for making most hues and it serves as a brightener. These are the people who bring sunshine into your life. They are usually spiritually strong and help guide you to God! These people are also great listeners and can get along with just about anyone. They are the easiest to have around and you will always feel better by having their sunny disposition near you.

Blue: cool, grounded, calm, and deep. This color is needed to create depth in a painting. Without blue you can't get black, brown, greens, or purples. These are the people you have deep conversations with. They are usually a calming factor in your life and help you stay connected to your bigger purpose and deeper self. When you are around them, you usually feel challenged and stretched. You can talk about deep things and even disagree, but you will feel like you've grown as a person after being around them.

Do you have a balance of the three primary colors?

Reflect: *is there a color lacking?* Maybe you avoid blues because you are scared to talk about deeper things. Perhaps you steer away from reds because you're afraid they might push you out of your comfort zone. Or maybe you keep yellows at arm's length because you've dismissed them as boring or too passive.

Take some time to write about the friends you have. Then describe what types of friends you'd like to add to your life. What good things could happen?

Which things frighten you? Example: *"I recognize that most of my friends are reds and yellows. I see that I'm attracted to people like myself. I might be a little intimidated by adding more blues onto my palette because I'm afraid I'm not as smart or they might find me superficial. I am going to be intentional about inviting more blues into my life— friends who can challenge me intellectually and spiritually."*

You need Fab Five friends too.

It was me, plus three and an art degree and it was during the recession of 2009. With the downturn of the economy and the divorce, I had to face the fact that we were going to lose our home—the house we had built together. It was a beautiful home I had designed, situated on five acres where I believed we would grow old together. Divorce isn't just losing a person or a relationship. It's losing all the dreams and ideas of the future you had imagined. I was losing everything and honestly, I didn't know how I was going to make it through. I needed a tribe, a palette of colorful people, to make a masterpiece out of this mess.

One of my Fab Five colors included my best friend, Catherine. She showed up to help me navigate all those yucky but necessary things you need to move through a divorce like finding a good lawyer, making a plan to move, creating a parenting plan for the kids and setting appropriate boundaries for a schedule. The irony was that just a year before, she was sleeping on *my* couch, bawling her eyes out after the discovery and sadness of her own husband's infidelity. My husband had even consoled her, talking about what a jerk her husband was for his selfish decisions— all the while he was doing the same thing. Catherine was a huge help in giving me the tools I needed to protect myself and the kids during this process. I'd say that Catherine's energy is cadmium yellow as she is generally bright and cheery, and you need a little "C-energy" in almost every aspect of life. She also gets things done. She showed up for long walks, coffee talks, family game nights, and some of the unpleasant things like house projects and court hearings. She always came with a smile and lots of energy, even in really difficult situations. Life with her is always better. Whatever I needed she was there, and I couldn't have done it without her.

My parents also showed up for me in a big way. My mom is a doer. She pushed me into action and kept me from crawling into a hole and wasting away. The more stressful things are, the more productive she is. She shows her love in service and, thus, picked up kids, cleaned my house, washed my clothes and even my car. She showed her love deeply and in practical ways. I'd say she was alizarin crimson during this time. A stabilizing factor to get me through.

I will never forget one night when I was staying alone. I was feeling extremely vulnerable and sad and so my dad drove from over an hour away and stayed with me. In the middle of the night, I started crying. It was a guttural cry, deep within my soul. My house was big, and he was sleeping on the bottom floor, but he still heard me, came up to my room and knocked on the door. He then came in and sat next to me. Just like his little girl, he held me and rocked me as I sobbed through all the pain, the loss, and the sadness. He cried too. I'll never forget his kindness and love in that moment for me. He was a grounding phthalo blue I needed in my life during that time.

Although I'd say that my sister, Danielle, is usually a blue for me, she showed up as a fiery cadmium red during this time. I needed justice and righteous anger to push me through. She can access red when somebody hurts her little sister, and the wrath of

Danielle is formidable. When I was waffling, I called her, and she'd give me a little slap of truth from Big Sis which always brought me clarity and gave me the strength to move forward in the right direction.

"No! He hasn't made any real changes," she said. "Stop listening to what he says and focus on what he *does!* Has he followed through on *any* of the promises he's made?" She reminded me of the truth and helped me see the parts I was blind to.

Grandma Dottie was another color on the palette. I'm assigning her ultramarine blue because we both loved New Mexico and that cobalt blue sky. She had started painting in her 70's and after realizing that the teachers in California weren't letting her do all the paintings she wanted, I got roped into being her art teacher after her plea of, "I don't have a lot of time on this planet to do these basic paintings and I want to be a real painter!" She helped to fill my life when the kids were at their dad's. I worried about being lonely, but instead I found myself on a plane for time with Grandma. When I arrived, she swept me into her art studio where we painted for hours, emerging only to eat or to buy more art supplies. My aunt, who lived next door, complained she didn't even know I had visited because Grandma kept me sequestered away in the studio. My grandpa sat on the porch smoking his pipe and jokingly complained about us hiding and working, but I could tell that he truly liked it. His eyes laughed when he saw us together. This was a color I hadn't expected, and it was so beautiful. As a wife and mother, I couldn't have spent all that time with my grandmother. As a single mom without the kids, I was free to enjoy it.

A good mix of friends opens up new opportunities.

Have you ever looked at an artist's palette? People usually imagine a palette before the artist has started painting. It's clean and the paint is neatly squeezed into little balls of color along the edges. Bright and cheery. Then the artist starts to paint. When mixing colors on the palette, it gets messy but there are also some unexpected and wonderful surprises. They are those mixes of colors that you didn't even know you could make—those "happy little accidents" as Bob Ross used to say. One of those happened at my grandmother's first solo art show. She was 81 years old. Of course, I had to fly down to Cali and be there for it. It was a huge success! She sold a few paintings, but the best part about it was seeing how proud she was of the work she created. She leaned over to me and whispered, "I'm just like Grandma Moses, but much more sophisticated and sexier, don't ya think?"

After the art show, she excitedly exclaimed, "You are in for a real treat! This is a full art weekend because my friend Father Gio, an Italian priest, is also doing an art show and all the proceeds will go toward building an orphanage in Uganda."

I was thrilled. This was going to be a weekend to remember. I loved spending time with my grandma, and I loved seeing art. The next day we were off to the bonus show with Fr. Gio. I walked into the U-shaped courtyard of the southwestern-style, stucco home and was overwhelmed with the amount of artwork that Fr. Gio had created. He had at least twenty-five large pieces of Italy, ranging from two to five feet, displayed throughout the house and set on easels along the deck. He used stucco and burlap to create texture like the Old-World painters of Italy. It was fascinating. On the bistro tables, there were bottles of wine with his paintings on them—this priest also had his own wine label. My eyes skimmed through the crowd searching for a man in black who wore the appropriate priestly attire. I couldn't find him anywhere, but I did notice a big crowd around a tanned man with steel blue eyes, wearing an unbuttoned white linen shirt, khaki shorts and Birkenstocks. He looked like Paul Newman in his mid-sixties. In one hand he was holding a cigar and in the other, a glass of wine. There is no way that this could be Fr. Gio!

Grandma Dottie proudly introduced me as her "professional artist granddaughter," which sparked the interest of Fr. Gio. Soon, we were talking shop about his paintings, and he pulled me into the garage to show me all of the materials he had used to create his pieces. I was curious as to this process of raising money for the orphanage and asked, "What if you don't make enough money?" He looked me straight in the eye and replied, "We sell a few pieces, we build a kitchen; we sell a few more, we build a house!" I loved this concept and his spirit. I was intrigued.

I bid on my favorite painting, one of an olive tree in grays, light blues and gold. Surprisingly, I won! *(I may have dropped the pen right after I signed it on the last call, so the other guy couldn't get his name in, but sometimes you've got to play a little dirty. I mean he already had bid on three other pieces for Pete's sake!)*

As Fr. Gio was signing it, I asked, "Hey, would you ever consider coming to Washington and doing a painting workshop for my Art-Women-Wine group?" At the time, I was running a little class out of my daylight basement.

He stopped signing, looked over the top of the painting, and asked, "Did you say art, women, and wine? I could be chill with that!" I giggled at how he used that college lingo with an Italian accent and thought, *My art ladies will eat this up!*

So, we planned for him to come in August. My art ladies were so excited to meet him and learn this Italian painting al fresco method! Little did I know that this unexpected color on my palette would change the whole trajectory of my life!

Chapter 3:
Art's Not for Wimps

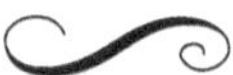

Bettie and her husband Les run a marina. You may have seen their moorage featured in the movie *Twilight.* A visit to their floating house on the Columbia River will reveal that they have an artistic eye for details, including a fishing hole with a glass flip-lid, which allows them and their grandkids to comfortably fish from their living room. Seriously, it is an amazing home.

You'll often find Bettie at her custom floating art studio moored nearby. She is an accomplished and prolific painter—selling her artwork on calendars, prints, coasters, and other curios. Her technique is sound. She doesn't need help in that area from me, yet she was a longtime student at Elida Art Studio and

Gallery. Her main motivation for coming to art class is social time. She's more interested in the coffee and mimosas (*Hold the orange juice, please!*) than the advice on how to complete an art piece.

With all those accolades, however, she still has trouble being courageous in her work. She is a careful, reserved painter and I know there is a confident, bold part of her that could be expressed more. Most of my conversations with Bettie about her paintings go something like this: "More, put more on, Bettie!" or "Trust yourself. Be brave and just lay that stroke down!"

Bettie inevitably says something like, "Ah, I knew you'd say that, but I couldn't do it. I chickened out!" I try reassuring her that, even if she overdoes it, the canvas will be forgiving. We can soften even the strongest stroke. But I remind her that she will miss out on the full impact of her painting if she fails to come in at the end and splash on those bold highlights.

One day, I decided to show her by taking some action. Sometimes you need to do something unexpected and maybe a little over the top to shock the system and help a concept to stick. With a black Sharpie pen, I wrote in big, scrawling letters on the canvas tablecloth next to her: "There is nothing you can do to screw this up!"

With my words written in ink before her, Bettie took a chance and went on to create some of her strongest pieces yet. Now, Bettie truly doesn't need me anymore. She still works as an independent artist in her enchanting studio, selling her works to vacationers and collectors alike. I get glimpses of her artwork when an event comes through my email or Facebook and feel a little burst of pride when I notice how she's much braver in her use of color. I'm so proud of Bettie for moving into the fearless artist I always knew existed. Art's not for sissies and cowards. Art is for the bold and daring. You must take some chances and see what may happen because the rewards can be huge.

Life isn't for wimps either.

My husband and I legally separated. Then, he stopped working and wouldn't pay child support. We put our house on the short-sell list for about a quarter of the price. Times were bad for a lot of people. We were no exception.

Our youngest, Weston, was just starting a three-day kindergarten that year so I only had a few days a week when I could work. Dreams of opening my own art studio had been bouncing around my brain for years but the timing was terrible. How would an art studio thrive in the middle of a recession and a divorce? The idea of "pursuing my passion" or "following my dream" seemed ludicrous.

Or did it? When I evaluated my strengths, I knew that teaching art was something that I was good at. I took tabs on what was already happening with art in my city and discovered that there were no art studios, galleries, or anything else art related. So, I decided to take a chance and advertised that I was offering an art camp that summer at my new studio in Camas.

"So where is your new studio?" People kept asking.

Demurely, I would reply, "I can't tell you—it's a surprise!" The truth was that my art studio didn't exist. I didn't even have a lead on any space. And the time was drawing dangerously close to summer. By the last week of school, I was still without a place to offer these art classes slated to start the following week.

Just a year before, I had been involved with the *Girl's Night Out* event in our town. It had taken place in this modern, fashionable, industrial space that was occupied by two other businesses. The business owners had opened the front area near the big windows for me to do a collective art project. At the end of the night, as I was cleaning my brushes in the oversized stainless-steel sink, I thought, *Wow, this place would be incredible as an art studio!* I added, *If I could ever have a space like this, it would be perfect!* At that time, neither of those businesses were planning to move. A year later, there were still no vacancies.

But somehow, word got out that I was looking for a space and the couple who owned one of the businesses in that space called me for a meeting. The studio that I had dreamed about with the big windows and the giant sink was going to be available and they were interested in subletting it to me. The rent was the exact amount that I could afford at that time, and the space was going to be available by—*drum roll, please*—Sunday. My first art camp started on Monday.

I signed the agreement, got myself a handwritten sign that read "Elida's Art Studio," and moved two folding tables and some chairs in on Sunday night. I emailed everyone the address for the big reveal. Less than twenty-four hours later, I taught my first art camp in my own studio. It was a dream come true.

It took a lot of guts to do it. But I knew that I had to take my brush, put a big dollop of paint on it, and just go for it! Lay it on thick. Trust myself and leap! That first step opened the door to many other opportunities. Within a year I could look back and see all the milestones I had passed. I built a strong, loyal following of clients and students and developed positive relationships within my city. Despite the chaos in my personal life, I didn't allow fear to get the better of me. Bravery was the better way.

As the teacher in the Book of Ecclesiastes says, there is a time for everything (Ecclesiastes 3:1 NIV), and there are times to be cautious and prudent. But most of us don't struggle with taking too many risks. We must fight against staying so safe instead. We just don't try enough things. We don't trust ourselves to reach for childhood dreams and personal passions. Just as in art, there are times to be bold. In our lives, we should be willing to sometimes grab a dollop of paint, a big brush, and paint the canvas of our lives with big strokes. Why? Well, because art, and life, isn't for wimps.

Be brave and bold in life.

Father Gio showed up for the workshop and started cooking pasta for everyone. As the women piled into the studio, the pasta was slopped onto plates, wine was poured heavily into their glasses, and I knew that this was going to be a different type of workshop than we had done before. The night was full of laughter and paint (including my ceilings and walls) but it was so much fun. I even forgot a little about my sadness and situation. I reminded the women to all come hungry the second night because I couldn't keep this guy out of the kitchen. So, the next night, they came hungry and there was more painting and pasta. At the end of the night everyone gathered back upstairs in the kitchen.

Sandy raised her wine glass and exclaimed, "Let's all gooooo to Italy!" and we all clinked our glasses and shouted "Wooohooo, oh yeah! Let's go!" Then the laughter, the chatting, and the drinking continued. I laughed and cheered with all of them but thought to myself, *There is no way that I could go to Italy right now while I'm going through a divorce and trying to raise these kids by myself! This is crazy talk!*

The next morning, I took Fr. Gio to the bus stop and I felt this deep sense of sadness as I was sending him onto his next adventure. I hugged him tight and then pulled back to look him in the eye and said, "You know, if I had done things differently, I would be more like you. I would be painting for causes and traveling the world."

His gaze met mine and he replied with a slight smile, "You know, Eli, there are two types of people in this world: those who talk about what they want to do and those who do it. Which one are you?" I felt the lump well up in my throat and I gulped back the tears. I forced a soft smile and gave him another hug and kiss on the cheek. As I was walking back to my car, I thought about his words and what they really meant. I thought about the clinking of glasses and the proclamation of going to Italy and how absurd the whole idea was. Then again, was it?

That night, after I got home, I sent an email to all my Art-Women-Wine ladies and asked a simple question: "Who was drinking too much wine and who is really serious about going to Italy?" What happened next really blew my mind.

Chapter 4:

Nobody Dies in Art Class

It was my first day teaching my Art Van-Go after-school art program. The kids excitedly filed into the classroom, eager to get started on their projects. All was going well until I noticed Emma, a sweet little girl, holding her breath and looking like she was about to cry. Her long, blond hair was neatly braided, and her outfit matched her pink shoes and bows. A quick look told me this wasn't her mother's doing. Emma had a personality that matched the bows with her shoes.

We were working with chalk pastels, which are a messy medium and difficult to control. If matching everything and making sure colors stay in the lines were important to little Emma, I could see why this activity might be hard for her. I squatted down so we could look at each other face-to-face and whispered: "Hey, let's take a few deep breaths." A tear spilled over and slipped down her cheek, but Emma nodded in agreement and breathed deeply. I quickly showed her how to blend the pastels with a few tricks and clean up those messy lines to crisp up the edges. Once she saw that it was fixable, she started to breathe normally again.

I checked in with a few other students as I strolled back to the front of the class, all the while thinking about Emma and her struggles. I guessed there were some other kids in class who felt similarly but were able to hide their tears. Suddenly, an inspiration came to me. I whipped around to face the class and commanded: "Everyone, drop your chalks and look up here for this very important announcement!"

The sudden command had the desired effect. All eyes were on me. I said, "I forgot to tell you the number one rule in Ms. Elida's art class." Dramatic pause. "The number one rule is...nobody dies in art class!" The kids stared blankly, waiting for an explanation. A few of them wiggled in their seats, their eyes dancing around the room, trying to make sense of this very strange declaration.

In my most theatrical manner, I pretended to mess up my drawing, wringing my hands and screaming, "Ohhhh, nooooooo! It's ruined! It's ruined! Wait! It's not just my painting. It's my heart! I think my heart might be giving out. I must be having an 'art attack!'"

Clutching at my heart, I dramatically fell onto the floor. Some of the younger kids got out of their chairs to check and see if I was dead. But the bigger kids caught on and had their own version of an 'art attack, falling to the ground with their tongues hanging out in feigned death throes.

Since that day, I always begin my art classes—for adults and children alike—with this rule. Why?

Because there is always at least one Emma in every class.

Starting with this rule helps students relax and not take their artwork too seriously. Instead, through some humorous overacting, I teach my students to distance themselves from their work. Here are some of the statements I often hear:

My artwork is ruined.

This is terrible.

Mine is the worst one.

This is unfixable!

If you have ever uttered statements like these, remember my number one rule: *nobody dies in art class!*

Most things we stress about aren't life or death.

The truth is that rule number one in Elida's art classes applies to life too—with a few caveats. *Nobody dies in life* doesn't really work, obviously, but most of the things we worry about never take place. And so, we spend a disproportionate amount of time stressing about events that don't occur.

I recently had a question about shipping artwork and decided to reach out to Marla, one of the managers at a previous art gallery where I used to show. They were the first to give me an opportunity to display my artwork as a budding artist, and our relationship had ended amicably and naturally. Once I had opened my own studio and gallery, it made sense to pull my artwork so I could hang it in my own space. Ironically, years later, the owners moved across the Columbia River from Portland, Oregon, to my little town of

Camas, Washington, and now have their gallery in my old space downtown.

My email to Marla was short, simply asking whom they would suggest using for shipping large art pieces, along with a few other questions. However, when I didn't receive a reply, my mind immediately raced to the worst conclusions: *Maybe that was out of line, like asking for a family recipe. Maybe that's a personal question. Maybe they are mad at me for leaving the gallery. Maybe they don't like my old art space. Maybe they resent me for something I didn't even know that I did.*

The "maybes" kept repeating in my head for a few days. I thought back over our history together, searching for something I could have done that would have offended them. I replayed every encounter and every conversation to find what I must have done wrong to make them ignore me like this. Then I began wondering who else might not like me; maybe I had offended the whole artistic community and just didn't know it.

After about three days of self-inflicted torture, I took a deep breath and sent a follow-up email to Marla. She immediately responded and apologized for missing my first email as she had just been busy that week. She was gracious and kind; all of those "maybes" were just false scenarios I had invited into my head. My simple little question had turned into a dying situation in my brain over a silly, missed email. I even needlessly lost sleep.

My first art director, Racquel, would often ask me, "Elida, is this a five-minute problem, five-day problem, or five-year problem?" The reality is that we often give a five-minute problem the emotional response of a five-year problem, but it doesn't have to be. As I'm getting older, I'm remembering to take my own advice by reminding myself, *Elida, you aren't going to die from this!* Instead, I take a big breath and resist jumping onto the Maybe Train.

We often give a five-minute problem the emotional response of a five-year problem.

Just after I sent that email about Italy to my Art-Women-Wine ladies, I switched into full time mom-mode for the school year. Fall is a sneaky season because just when you get into a new school routine, the holidays are there without any warning. It starts with Halloween, next Thanksgiving, Christmas, and then New Year's Day comes barreling around the corner.

Suddenly, I was facing my first Christmas without my kids. I was so busy with keeping up with all our schedules that I didn't plan for this inevitability, which I had long known. Before I knew it, I was sobbing.

It wasn't just the prospect of facing Christmas alone. I had fast-forwarded myself into thinking, *Where am I going to sit at the future wedding when Emily, Caleb or Weston get married? Will his family sit with my family on the bride's side or separately? Who is going to have the graduation party? Do we have a joint party? What about pictures? How do you write all of that on those fancy invitations you send out?*

Do you see the spiral here? One of the best things I learned at this time was to stop looking at ALL the holidays for the rest of my life and instead just focus on what was next. I was not going to die from this, and in fact, I was going to grow from it if I could change my perspective. Instead of getting depressed and being alone without my kids for Christmas (which was plan A), what if I looked at this time as a gift for me to have some freedom and visit my Grandma Dottie for a Swedish Art Getaway where we could paint and play together? California is usually much nicer in the winter. Getting a little sun and quality time with my grandparents seemed the perfect solution. I booked my ticket for Cali and every time I thought of that week alone at Christmas, it shifted my feelings about it from dread to excitement and joyful anticipation. I wasn't sure if I was more excited for the first week with the kids or the second week with my grandparents.

* * *

The second rule in Ms. Elida's art class is: There are no mistakes in art, just different directions.

Art is scary for people who mistakenly think they must follow a set of rules. They believe they need to make something look exactly how they see it in their minds or copy specifically what they see by looking at a picture or an object and, if they can't, well then, the life-definitive statement comes into their minds: I must not be good at art. Art is frightening for those who believe that the world is divided between people who are naturally good at art and people who are innately bad at art. They approach the canvas like it is a magic mirror that will reveal some terrible truth about themselves.

I hear statements like, "I can only draw stick figures" or "Mrs. Green told me that art isn't my thing." I usually respond with something like, "Mrs. Green doesn't get to dictate your life anymore. She's probably dead by now!" If you remove the expectation of what your painting should look like, quiet the judgments you've heard or said about your artistic self and open your mind to the idea that everything you make can be made into something else, it shifts something fundamental within you. In almost every other school subject there is a right answer or right way to do it, but in art, you can do something very wrong and still make it into something spectacular.

A few years ago, I was painting a flamenco dancer. As a creative thinker, I like to multitask, so I was talking on the phone, listening to the radio, and painting at the same time. I wasn't really paying much attention to my painting when I discovered that it was dripping. *What the heck?*

I quickly yelled, "Gotta go! I'll call you back." I threw the phone aside and assessed the situation. My dancer was melting away on the canvas. It reminded me of the scene from *The Wizard of Oz* when the wicked witch gets water thrown on her and she squeals "I'm melting, I'm melting," as she crumbles to the ground and disappears. My poor dancer was doing the same thing—she was dripping and sliding right off the canvas before my eyes. I could have cried or, even worse, broken my number one rule and had an 'art attack and died. Instead, I stepped back and thought, *Wait, she's not a dancer. She's a mountain and a waterfall and there's a little river coming toward me!* I quickly switched plans and began painting an abstract landscape.

It turned out to be one of my favorite paintings. In fact, I liked it so much that it spawned an entire series of abstract landscapes. Eventually, I returned to painting my dancers, but if I had forced that painting into what I had aimed for it to be, or if I had scrapped it, I would have missed out on one of the best painting series of my career.

When you're facing a huge mistake in your life, no matter who made it, look for how you can steer it in a different direction.

The trip to California ended up being exactly what I needed. My grandparents pampered me. On New Year's Eve, I found myself at a ritzy restaurant where we ate and drank and danced until the ball dropped on New York City. I was blessed that my grandparents had a wide collection of friends (their palette had all the right colors to make a lovely life), most of them much younger and with diverse cultures and interests.

If I were home with the kids, I would have put them to bed on time and then watched the ball drop from my couch. I might have had a little glass of bubbly, but it wouldn't have had Father John dancing on the floor exploding with his jolly laugh. It wouldn't have had the sparkle and pizazz that always seemed to accompany Grandma Dottie with her sassy, dark eyes and effervescent personality. It wouldn't have had my grandfather, out of his element whenever he wasn't in his study but could exert himself to deeply enjoy a moment like this when it presented itself. It was the perfect New Year's Eve celebration and the end to a fabulous week. As the plane swam into the clouds, I felt rested, loved, and rejuvenated. Even now, I look back on that time with a smile.

When I was able to change directions versus focusing on the sadness and badness of the situation, I ended up having one of the most special Christmas holidays of all time. Search for the opportunities versus pining away for your loss. It changes everything. I couldn't see at that time that these moments with my grandparents were fleeting. They were precious. I had no idea then what was looming, but from where I stand, I realize I experienced a rich and deeply special time with my grandparents.

* * *

The third and final rule in Ms. Elida's art class is: *Have fun.*

Creating is as ancient as we are. God is a master artist and created us to create as well. It keeps us in balance. It helps in other endeavors. It opens pathways in our minds. But creating is also an end in itself and, if done right, it is fun! If it isn't fun, it is because of the expectations we put on ourselves as to how the artwork will turn out. What I'm trying to proclaim from the mountaintops with these rules—and will continue preaching until I die—is that *art shouldn't be stressful; it should be fun!*

Do you realize that most artists, like the real McCoys—the bona fide, legitimate professional ones (I'm being sarcastic here; you are a real artist, too, you just might not know it yet)—struggle with liking their paintings? I've sold thousands and thousands of dollars' worth of work and still, I get my painting to a point to where I'm satisfied. Soon after I have sold the painting or moved on to another piece, I look back and think, *Dang, I could have done*...this, or that—whatever it is that could be better. You're not alone in judging your work. You're in good company. What you need to do, though, which other "real" artists have learned to do, is acknowledge how you could have made it better, accept how you finished it, and let it go. The truth about having created is that when you are done with your painting or other creative endeavor, you need to remind yourself that the piece was as good as you could do *at that time.* It's not meant to be perfect. It's meant to be a *marker* for yourself to see where you are. Take off the expectations. Be surprised at the outcome. Repeat. You can always paint over it. You can always donate it or hang it in the garage. The important part is that you are having fun in the process of creating. You are present and enjoying the process without putting too many expectations on yourself or the work.

Would this little art lesson translate to something as devastating as a divorce? Could I somehow find a way to have fun when my heart was broken? That trip to Grandma and Grandpa's at Christmas helped me get through a difficult holiday, but what about the rest of my life? I looked at the future and it stretched out before me with me walking along in it ... alone. Could I have fun while I was alone?

I sat down at my desk and opened my email and when I glanced through the list, my heartbeat faster. Many of the women had responded with genuine interest. It wasn't just the Prosecco. They really wanted to go to Italy. I was surprised and excited thinking about the possibility of going. I thought about what Father Gio had said,

There are those who talk about what they want to do and those who do it. Which one are you?

My sadness lifted a little and my mind wandered. Italy with its sunny climate, it's fashionable and beautiful people, and its glorious food. The movie, *Eat-Pray-Love,* had recently come out and I dreamt of eating a whole margarita pizza by myself in Naples or walking the cobblestone streets of Rome. Wait, is that a hot Italian guy giving me a lift on his vespa to take me out for dinner and gelato? Why yes, it is!

But I had zero experience organizing or leading tours anywhere. Yet, there were a handful of women who were genuinely interested in going to Italy with me! That sounded like a lot of fun. I took a deep breath, smiled, and started searching for hotels and transportation.

Chapter 5:

Go for Tiger-ish

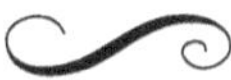

I was hosting a Christmas paint party for my favorite coffee shop. Because I frequent this shop quite often (almost daily), I know most of the gals who work there. The staff wanted to paint a nostalgic red truck with a flocked Christmas tree hanging off the back. It's a well-known scene for Christmas and incredibly popular but the task before me was daunting. I had to teach a group—many of them without drawing or painting experience— how to draw a 1950s Chevy, paint it, add the tree, add a foreground, and splatter snow within a two-hour time frame.

Before I began, I said, "Hey, everyone, we are going to paint something vintage, red, and truck-ish. It may be an El Camino, it may be a monster truck, it may be a short bed or a long bed, but it will be truck-ish." I got a giggle out of the group, and I hoped the joke broke the tension and the expectation that everyone was going to have a recognizable 1950s Chevy. After the lesson got going, I noticed one truck looked more like an old Buick family wagon. The front was as big as the back, and you couldn't really tell which was which. Still, there was something so endearing about that instead of helping Nissa change it, I showed her a few tricks to keep going with the style she naturally was doing. She was completely aware it wasn't at all like the model I was demonstrating, but she chuckled, shrugged, and said, "It's truck-ish, right?"

It was a fabulous night, and in the end, we laid out everyone's "trucks" together for a picture. Despite their differences, everyone agreed that the collage of trucks was charming, especially together, and that even if they weren't perfect, they were truck-ish!

In scientific drawings, it's imperative to copy exactly because medical students will rely on the images to prepare for serious duties like surgery or diagnoses. Exactitude has its uses, but it is not the purpose of art in my classes—nor is it the only definition of a good artist.

There's a wonderful children's book called *Ish* by Peter H. Reynolds. The premise behind the book demonstrates how the main character discovers that creativity is a lot more than getting things right. I often tell new students that everyone's picture will look "bike-ish," "llama-ish," or whatever we are making. It will look something like that, but not exactly like it. No one's art piece will be a good copy of mine because we all see and create differently. People often feel that if they can't duplicate what I'm doing, then their painting isn't good. They compare their rendition to mine or their neighbor's, and it becomes a competition, not an enjoyable process.

I first heard of "ish" from an artist named Angie. We were both in our mid-thirties when I heard about her—our sons were about the same age, and we both knew Fr. Gio. Angie was an acrylic and pastel artist. A few years prior, a tumor burst in Angie's brain. They raced her to the hospital where she went into a coma and underwent immediate surgery. When she finally awoke, she discovered she was paralyzed from the neck down. One of the first things she asked for was a slice of pizza from her favorite restaurant and to "get me a brush and my paints. I think I can paint with my mouth!"

Over the next few weeks and months Angie continued to paint with her mouth, improving her craft slowly. She created a book called *Tiger-ish,* full of paintings she created after her paralysis, with captions that explained how each piece was a little *"ish"* in its own way.

Eventually, Angie passed away. When I went to the memorial service, I heard another story about Angie that helps to illustrate why it's important to let go of our high expectations of how our paintings should look. After Angie had passed, Angie's mother-in-law asked her grandsons which paintings they wanted to keep in their rooms as a reminder of their mom. Hunter, the youngest, chose an unusual painting—it had a big splash of color through the middle of it.

She asked, "Why this one?"

He replied, "I remember when my mom painted this painting. She was painting in the kitchen, and she told my brother and me not to run around or rough house because she was painting and needed to focus. We didn't listen very well. I was running from my brother. I tripped and hit my mom's arm while she was in the middle of painting. It made a big stroke of paint across the piece. I felt bad, and I said I was sorry. She just looked at me with a smile and said, 'It's okay, Hunter. I think this painting needed this today. I would have never thought to make such a big stroke of green, so you helped me make it special!' She finished the painting with my accident in it. So that one is the most special for me."

I think of how, in life, I have been like Hunter, running around and messing up God's masterpiece—and he's just smiled down at me and said, "It's okay. I wanted this massive green stripe in this painting, Elida!"

He must allow a lot of things in our lives to be "ish," giving us the freedom to paint our lives with childlike enthusiasm. He's patient when we really mess things up and works those mistakes into the canvas of our lives.

God allows a lot of things in our lives to be "ish," giving us the freedom to paint our lives with childlike enthusiasm.

I finalized the dates, collected the money, and launched the first Art-Women-Wine tour with the intrepid Fr. Gio as guide. Twelve women. Twelve days and a priest in Italy!

Fr. Gio had led dozens of tours for college students. He knew the areas we were going to tour well so I relied on him for most of the planning. He guided me to which accommodations were best and which modes of transportation made sense from place to the next. What I didn't know, however, is that what worked for college students might not translate to middle-aged women.

When we arrived at the "chateaus in Rome," I discovered that they were trailers at a campground. Then, Father Gio—who loves spontaneity and surprise— convinced everyone to jump on a train to go south to Naples, even though I already had paid for our train and accommodations in Florence. The women were all chattering excitedly and even planning their shopping excursions to Naples, or a day trip to Pompeii, and I knew that if I didn't take control in this moment, we would lose our hotel and money for the train. And, by the way, what was Gio's plan once he had us all down to Naples? I clinked my wine glass with my fork, cleared my throat, then went through the reasons why it was a bad idea to follow Fr. Gio south and listed out the reasons why it was a good idea to stick to the original plan. The group finally conceded and onto Florence we went.

When we got on the train, I asked Gio if the women needed to know their assigned seats. He shrugged his shoulders and said, "Nah, just get these ladies on the train and we'll be good to go." The women got on and sat down but when the other travelers started to come onto the train, they started asking for their seats. Soon we were all standing up and scrambling around, trying to figure out which seat was which. Later, I realized why Gio had been so flippant about the assigned seats. When he led students on a trip by train, there was likely a large amount—like fifty to a hundred students—so, yeah, it didn't matter where they sat because the college had probably bought the entire train car for the group. Things did not get much better when we arrived in Florence and learned that the hotel downtown was a hostel, and the apartments were just rooms with bunk beds. We were six women in each room, sharing one bathroom. Hoisting middle aged women up to a top bunk was not what I had in mind.

Then there were some funny things like when Gail caught her hair on fire with her hair dryer because

Europeans use a higher voltage system than we do. The adapter wasn't enough to keep it from burning out! Finally, we make it to the small village of Cagli. I thought I could at least relax here because this is where we planned to do most of our painting. That was one thing I knew how to do well! But Gio insisted he be the one to get the art supplies for the group. I had questioned him about it in Florence as I had seen plenty of supply stores, but he assured me we'd find great art materials in Cagli. So, it was our first night to paint and Fr. Gio pulls out children's Crayola watercolor paint sets (later, I found that he bought them from the grocery store). I think my mouth dropped open in disbelief. We used what we had in the moment, and everyone was flexible and fun. Still, I promised the ladies an extended art session with real paints back at the studio when we returned from Italy.

I had to take a deep breath, tell myself to relax, and say, *This Italy tour was tour-ish!* I had already warned the ladies that this was my first tour, and I didn't have any experience to speak of, so please be understanding! And they were, at least most of them. We had made it to Italy, but it certainly wasn't what I had expected nor was it what anyone expected. Yet, there was nothing like that first tour. If I hadn't just stepped out in faith and gone for it, even with all the imperfections and snafus, well, you'll see where it led me.

I didn't mention how many things we got right. Even though it was a far cry from a professionally led tour, it was a heck of a lot of fun. There were dancing, smoking cigarettes on the porch of our "chateaus" (even though none of us smoke) and drinking wine until the late night hours. There was also a romance with a Florentine leather shop owner that was another turn in my story (don't worry, you'll get the deets later). Yes, it was an amazing adventure, and I would have missed it, we all would have missed it, if I had waited until everything was perfect. It was an Italy tour-ish and it was far from flawless, but we had made a dream come true.

On one of the last breakfasts in Italy, Father Gio leaned back in his chair, sipping his espresso and reading the Italian newspaper. He shook the paper a little, looked over the top of his reading glasses and half whispered in his Italian-laced English, "We've got a lot of good sh*# going on here. We should DO THIS AGAIN." My eyes widened as I slurped the last bit of foam from my cappuccino con doppia caffè. I licked my lips and said, "I agree we've got a lot of good stuff happening, but what do you mean?

Do you think we should do another tour to Italy?" My mind was racing now. I was struggling to understand. He shook the paper a little harder this time, licked his finger and turned the page, then retorted, "Have you ever heard of the Amalfi Coast?"

Chapter 6:

Don't Spread the Negative Goo

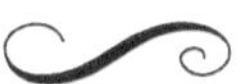

I was teaching an artist-in-residency program for our local fifth graders. These years are a tumultuous time when they are torn between childhood and being thrust into adolescence. I remember my daughter, Emily, at this age, sliding across the gym floor on her volleyball knee pads while wearing mascara. Junior high or middle school is imminent, and they are already jockeying for positions in whichever group they will be a part of. They also become hyper aware of whose work is best. This comparison opens the door for tearing down each other or themselves.

In every 5th grade class, there's always one who will start talking negatively about his or her painting, and today it was Liam. He spouted out, "I hate my picture, and this art project sucks."

If I didn't do something quickly, the negativity would spread throughout the room like a virus. I shouted, "Oh no, stop right there! Did all of you see that?" Everyone's eyes turned toward me as I raced over to Liam and looked closely at him like he had just puked. In a shrill voice, I said, "Oh no! Liam has opened the gate for the negative goo! Blub, blub, blub, blub." I moved my hands over the top of the kids' heads and down to the floor, waving my hands like an ocean while saying "Blub, blub, blub, blub, blub." Then I covered my ears and wailed, "Nooo, noooooooo! Please stop the negative goo from spreading!"

They started laughing except for a few of the cool kids who crossed their arms and tried to pretend they were mad. But in the end, I won them over and they all chuckled because I went so overboard making the goo sounds around them until they succumbed to the silliness. Once the entire class was making negative goo sounds, I showed them how they could spread positive pixie dust. "Puff, puff, puff," I chanted while traipsing around the room like a floating fairy, singing out positive things about each of the kids' paintings.

"I love how Lindsay used pink as a highlight color…la, la, la…puff, puff, puff. Oh, look at Jeremiah's use of blue, it looks like it's glowing! Puff, puff, puff, puff!" Soon, everyone was saying positive things, and the whole atmosphere of the classroom changed. By the end of the class, they were even mocking my "puff, puff, puff" sounds as they expanded their fingers open in the air, saying, "Marvelous, darling, I love your color!" Everyone was smiling and having fun; the most negative of them didn't stand a chance against all the positive energy, even if some of the comments bordered on sarcasm.

Have you ever met a Negative Nelly? It seems that no matter what you try and do, she always has something bad or negative to say. Negativity is highly contagious. Just as I must stop the spread of the negative goo in the classroom, I also find myself stopping it with people in my regular life too. My first line of defense is to avoid negative people, if possible, surrounding myself with friends and family who lift me up, inspire me, and pray for me. But what about those people whom you can't avoid? Maybe it's a family member or someone at your workplace. When it is impossible to limit time with a negative person, plan on how to protect yourself with positive pixie dust.

Don't let negative people infect you with their negativity.

I kept thinking about Fr. Gio's suggestion that we lead another tour. I wrote down all sorts of "Notes to Self" about what went wrong—the chateaus that were trailers, having a clear itinerary, train tickets for specific seats, European electrical output versus American, and when and where to get art supplies. When I stepped back to assess them, I asked *Are they five-minute problems or five-year problems*? Really, they were all quite manageable when I thought about it. On the next tour, I could avoid all those mistakes. I could revamp our Art Tour-ish into something a little more refined. What if, instead of staying at hostels and "chateaus," we stayed in beautiful boutique hotels and modern apartments? And what about the Amalfi Coast? I leaned back in my chair and remembered the scene from *Under the Tuscan Sun* and that hottie from Positano, yes, that beautiful man she had a romance with but also that gorgeous scenery, overlooking the sea. Wasn't that the Amalfi Coast? Sign me up!

Already word had spread through our little community and people were asking, "When's the next tour?" With all the failings, despite everything being less than perfect, the women still had a blast and the memories and the moments they shared showed far more enthusiasm and trust than I felt I deserved. So, I started to plan a tour that was a little more fitting for mature adults and less frat-house style like Father Gio had organized before. Everything was clicking along until... I got the email.

One of my original travelers was disgruntled. She was one of my art students who joined at the last minute, hadn't been completely honest on her questionnaire, and she was high maintenance because she insisted on venturing off alone all the time and refused to really become a part of the group. When we got to the last town on the tour, I asked if anyone needed a room alone, and her roommate, Christie, threw up her hand immediately. Later, Christie shared she hadn't had much sleep the entire trip up to this point due to the erratic behavior by her roommate. I had no idea that these issues were happening and did my best to solve the problem by giving them both their own rooms. Also, while on the trip, this discontented customer made some strange complaints. I investigated, tried to resolve things to the best of my ability, and moved on. It wasn't until after we were home, getting settled into my normal routine when she sent me the vicious letter. The accusations and the character assassinations were what hurt the most.

As I read through it again, however, I realized that what she was mad about was that the tour was a success. She seemed to be lashing out due to jealousy rather than complaining. I had made huge disclaimers that this was my first tour, I was new and relying heavily on Fr. Gio's expertise. But if I could read through the seething anger, I could see she wanted to ruin my plans of doing any future tours.

I talked it over with Fr. Gio and went through everything she had accused me of to see if any of it was true. As I had learned from my earlier lessons, I knew that not everyone liked me nor was I going to be everyone's favorite, but I didn't see this coming. I sent her back an email and asked if we could meet in person to talk through her concerns. I've discovered that unstable and angry people don't like to deal with anyone who is ready to solve problems and advocate for themselves. They make grandiose accusations on social media or through text messaging, but when it is time for face-to-face negotiations, poof! They disappear. I've never heard from her since.

Later I heard that she tried opening her own studio and was recruiting some of my Art-Women-Wine ladies to join her. *Puff! Puff! Puff!* I sprinkled my positive pixie dust by wishing her well and encouraged others to join her studio if that was a better fit for them. Then, I moved forward, not allowing her jealousy to ruin my plans or my life. Fortunately, it didn't stop me from planning the next tour to the Amalfi Coast, then to Tuscany, and another to Greece.

The good news is that I've only had to deal with Negative Nelly travelers a few times. It was during the first week in Italy when we dealt with our second Negative Nelly. It became apparent that this traveler had significant mood swings. One moment we were the best tour guides in the world, and she loved, loved, loved us! The next minute she was yelling at me because I didn't remember her favorite drink. We were leading a group of twelve, and I managed all the food orders while keeping track of each person's dietary needs—allergies, gluten-free, vegetarian, pescatarian, paleo, vegan, and food aversions. Yep, I deal with the "I don't like potatoes unless they are fried in a certain type of oil" allergy too. It's a total pain, but I do it every single trip. So, yes, I sometimes forget if a traveler takes sugar or cream in their coffee! After our last meal of that first week—and our resident Negative Nelly's explosive behavior—I had a meeting with her. I gave her three choices: 1) Stay with us for the next tour with a change in attitude. 2) Stay with us for the next tour but do her own thing. 3) Go home early on her dime.

When you don't put up with negativity, people adjust quickly. She decided to go on the rest of the tour with us, choosing to do her own thing on most days but sometimes staying with the group when she felt like it. Great! Problem solved. Don't compound others' negativity with your own negative response. Being negative is a choice! That's right—your view and your response to any circumstance is a decision that you get to make.

I remember a time I was in an argument with my ex-husband. He was standing over me and yelling in my face, spewing abusive things at me. I could feel everything around me get very still and, although I was looking right at him, nothing was coming through. I was totally at peace. A quiet smile broke over my face and he just kept going. Finally, in a desperate attempt to force me to react, he yelled, "Are you even listening to me?"

Calmly, I said, "I don't have to listen to you anymore. I really don't care what you think or what you have to say, and nothing you can say or do will hurt me anymore." I turned and walked away. I felt a powerful, angelic presence. It was the first time I had stood up to him in a way that wasn't out of control or frantic. I was anchored in God. I've always thought how cool it would be to have a superpower; in that moment I felt like a superhero. I was like Neo in the Matrix when the bullets were coming at him, and everything slowed down as he did a gymnastic backbend in his super cool black leather suite. I get that I wasn't wearing any leather that day. My superhero outfit often included yoga pants, a T-shirt, and flip flops, but you know, metaphorically speaking I was leathered up, I was doing some serious backbend magic moves to avoid that negativity. Resisting negativity is perhaps one of the greatest superpowers in existence.

Spreading positive pixie dust is a choice, as well. Susan was one of our art tour travelers; she had never been to Italy on one of my tours and was so excited about her upcoming chance. When we arrived on that sunny peninsula, she greeted me every morning with a smile, saying, "Elida, if I forget to tell you later, today was the best day *ever*!" She didn't even know what was on the agenda or what we had planned for that day, but she had already decided to make that day in Italy a great day—and for Susan, it was. I wish we had women like Susan on every single trip. I wish we had a "Susan App" to tell us just how great our day is going to be. In a world where negative goo spreads quickly across social media, the news, and the people around us, we need lots of positive pixie dust.

***Puff! Puff! Puff!* I sprinkled my positive pixie dust by wishing her well and encouraged others to join her studio if that was a better fit for them.**

Shortly after Grandma Dottie's art show and the start of my tours to Italy, she got cancer. Again. For the third time. She had already beaten breast cancer two other times in her life and didn't even have breasts for that nasty disease to grow in anymore, but it found its way to her stomach and colon. I was so angry. "Why, why, why did this have to happen? She has already endured so much pain. This wasn't fair!"

We kept our painting dates on the calendar, despite her diagnosis. Painting and creating was an important positive for her during this time. On one of my visits to Cali, she nonchalantly told me, "Hey, so I have this little thing I need to do tomorrow for a few hours. It's kind of boring, so you might want to bring a book, but afterwards we are going to meet up with my friends at my favorite bar to parrrrr-tayyyyy!" Sounded like a good plan to me.

The next day, I packed my water bottle and book and slid into the silver Mercedes Benz. Grandma Dottie looked fabulous, with her gorgeous white hair about mid-length, designer sunglasses, and some red lipstick. She looked as if we were going out to a special event. Instead, she pulled into the parking lot of the hospital. She smiled and said, "Remember, we've got something super fun after!"

As we walked in, I noticed all the sick and depressed-looking people. She checked in and walked to the back where there was a large room with lots of different people all hooked up to machines. It became clear that she was here for a chemo treatment. She sat down in the chair and rolled up her sleeve and then flashed me that million-dollar smile. "Don't worry, it goes by fast and soon we will be having some fun drinks!"

Her light and enthusiasm began to spread throughout the room. I could see the pixie dust of her joy floating to others. She smiled, made small talk, bragged about me and my art, and shared jokes and stories for the next four hours. I was amazed at how her presence and enthusiasm shifted the environment in the entire room. I never got to read a page from my book because the entertainment and conversation was much more interesting. Soon we were skipping out and headed to the bar to meet up with her friends.

She then confessed, "I've got tonight, Elida, where I will feel pretty good. Tomorrow is another story." She was teaching me to find joy in the moment and teaching me to embrace the reality of facing pain. I was taking some "Notes to Self" again, but this time it was for my life. I believed I had made it through my anguish with my divorce. Clearly, I had suffered enough already and shouldn't have to go through it again. Little did I know, like Grandma with that cancer attacking her repeatedly, grief and suffering would find me in the future. But that night, we drank bubbly and partied, finding joy in the here and now.

Chapter 7:

Everyone Sucks When They Start

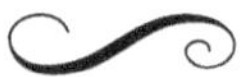

It was the first time that my mom, Shirley, had ever painted with me. The only reason she was with me at my Edenwild Art Retreat was because I made up some excuse about how I really needed her help and wanted some company for the drive. The reality was that I just wanted her to have a weekend away with some fabulous women and great food—and to finally paint with me. My mom is an excellent teacher, practically a legend in our community. She is also very creative musically, playing the piano, organ, and accordion, and she can even sing. She directed plays in both our church and at school, often acting in them as well. She loves history, travel, adventures, and Jesus (not in that order), but she has always avoided drawing or painting.

I'm sure it didn't help that when I was five, sitting in a church pew, I figured out she couldn't draw—and she realized that I knew it. I had taken the offering envelope out of the slot in front of me and carefully opened all the edges so that I had the most paper surface to work with. Then I slid the paper over to her and whispered, "Could you please draw me a dog?" She sat there for a minute with a forced smile and then proceeded to draw an animal of sorts that looked nothing like a dog—maybe a wombat, raccoon, or opossum—but not a dog. I'm sure she caught the confused and deflated look on my face as I took my paper back. I remember wondering, *How is she not good at this? She is supposed to be better at everything than I am.* I never asked for help in drawing again. And my mother never offered.

Fast forward forty years later, my mom sat in a front seat at the retreat where I was teaching everyone to paint a calla lily. I went through the whole spiel of my three rules in art class and reminded everyone to give themselves a lot of grace. I repeated and reiterated about being positive and just enjoying the process. Still, the most negative person in the group was my mom:

"Oh, wow, this is terrible."

"Goodness gracious, this looks bad. Look at Tisha's—hers looks so nice."

"Elida, I messed this up so much, I don't think you can fix it."

It was nonstop negativity! I wanted to pinch the back of her arm like she used to do to me when I misbehaved in church and tell her quietly in her ear, "If you don't knock it off, I will walk you right out of here and spank your bottom!" But I couldn't. So, we limped along through the lesson and the next. She still hated her paintings. Even with all my help and encouragement, she often asked me if I could just paint over them.

I reminded her that this was her first time painting! First paintings are rarely good and certainly don't look like those of more seasoned painters. Why would she expect hers to look like some of the others when they had all been painting for a long time? "Mom, the first one always sucks! You have to do this piece first so you have something to look back on and see your progress." I felt like my life lessons from painting fell flat with Mom, even after experiencing so much success with other would-be painters.

But the next year, she came back. Since she already knew a little from the year before, she was a *teensy-weensy* bit more confident. And she was a bit quieter, too. My sister came for the first time and was putting out the negative vibes, so it gave my mom some freedom to be a little bit more positive. Her pieces improved and she even took them home. Later in the week, she texted me a picture showing her calla lily painting hanging up in the downstairs bathroom. Her message said, "Look what I hung up! Even Dad says it's pretty good!" My heart filled with joy to see this breakthrough. Since she can barely sit still for a class, I doubt my mom will ever take up painting as a profession or even a hobby, but I'm thankful she was able to let go of enough of her negative ideas to enjoy the process of painting.

My first painting class for adults was a six-week course. The first two classes were drawing only and the last four weeks focused on painting. I asked my four students to give me feedback for the next round. They all said, "Can we skip the drawing and just paint?" I knew that drawing was a necessary part of painting, but I also knew it was a more difficult and time-consuming skill to learn. Women were coming for a break. They were exhausted; life was already hard, and they just needed to paint for fun. The technical part could come later.

Kelly had been painting with me for years. Being a self-proclaimed "numbers person" meant that she sometimes struggled with loosening up and being free in her painting. But Kelly was determined and stuck with it, eventually developing her own style, creating a connection with one of her daughters (who also enjoyed painting), and even selling her work. There was a point in her development, however, when she plateaued and decided she needed some drawing lessons. Later, after attending a workshop, she reported, "Elida, I seriously would have walked right back out of that drawing studio had I gone there before painting with you. It was scary and overwhelming, but the confidence I've gained in my painting kept me going. I even got some compliments from the head teacher and my work is improving. Drawing isn't so scary anymore, but had I started out trying to draw, it would have been too hard and too much."

Kelly learned an important lesson in painting: Not only did she learn to paint, but she also learned that she is capable of learning something new. Going through the painful process of being the uncoordinated newbie gave her the confidence to try a drawing class and take her artistic skills to a new level. Kelly's work continues to improve. She created a beautiful portrait of her dad, capturing his essence in a way that could have only been done through the extra training she did with the drawing classes.

Now, when I teach Art-Women-Wine classes, I don't start with a lesson in drawing because it's too overwhelming. People can't handle sucking when they begin. Painting has enough forgiveness built into it that it eases people into the state of being a learner. Truth be told, you're not good when you start. No one is. And the creative process is so personal that when you see a terrible rendition of something you did it feels like it reflects on your worth.

It's easy for me, as a teacher, to glibly say, "Everyone sucks when they start." I developed my artistic talent from a young age when we are used to learning new things. But I sometimes push myself as an artist into new areas so I can also experience what it's like to suck. One summer, I attended a plein air painting workshop in Central Oregon. In general, I am a studio artist. Plein air artists are a different breed. It's like sand volleyball players versus gym volleyball players—it's the same sport but a totally different game. I showed up to the outdoor class with my acrylic paints, a fluorescent orange T-shirt, and a little travel easel. I forgot a hat, adequate water supply, or really anything anybody else had, including the type of paint you should use. I was not prepared.

My first discovery was that most plein air artists are oil painters because the paint stays moist despite the weather. Acrylics, on the other hand, dry quickly. So, if you are in the desert, which I was, on a one-hundred-degree day, which it was, your paints dry the moment you squirt them from the tube onto your palette, which they did.

Next, I got sick and had diarrhea and was in the outhouse for most of the afternoon. Do you know how embarrassing it is to have the runs and in the only honey bucket for miles? *Knock, knock, knock. "Are you almost done in there?"* Finally, I got a heat stroke and almost died (not literally, but I certainly didn't feel well). So, here I was at this plein air workshop, a professional artist who looked so not professional. The other artists were all equipped with the latest easels, paints, and gear, and they were also name-dropping about their sanseis. *Hi, I'm Carla and I study under Master Important out of San Francisco.*

I tried taking deep breaths and giving myself a little grace, but my paints were drying faster than I could get them on my canvas and the wind was blowing my palette paper over. I wondered why everyone was dressed in such boring clothes, all brown and gray, until one of the instructors asked me not to wear my colorful T-shirt the next day because the bright color was reflecting onto my canvas! Who knew? Somehow, I managed to make it through the weekend. The pieces weren't my best work, but I was proud of them, mostly because I allowed myself to be a novice and do something completely out of my element.

We are quick to tell our kids to try new things, and yet, as adults, we steer away from anything that pushes us too much. If we aren't good at something immediately, we just don't do it. But the truth is we are all novices when we first start anything.

A few years ago, I was training for a triathlon. I could run and bike without a problem, but the swim was a different story. My doggy paddling or backward stroke probably wouldn't get me too far in a race. My volleyball friend, Raquel, convinced me to take a swimming class with her. I thought if we could do it together it wouldn't be too bad. I showed up to the club pool with my bikini on and ready to "rock and roll, baby!" Then, I noticed that all the other students had swim caps, goggles, and one-piece swimsuits. My friend saw me sporting my bikini, so she pulled me aside and said, "Hey, I figured you might not have everything, so I have a few extra things for you to borrow, Elida." She had a one-piece Nike swimsuit for me to wear. After changing, I put on my swim cap (sideways) and strapped on my goggles. As I walked out to class, the instructor told me to go to lane one. I climbed in the pool alongside a hundred-year-old granny who feared the water and a man so fat I was worried he might have a heart attack just floating.

The instructor pointed to the middle lane and said, "Please watch Raquel show us the first strokes for our class today." I squinted my eyes and realized this was my friend. She clearly was a good swimmer and already the teacher's pet! We started with all our different strokes. Then it was time to try swimming with our heads underwater, practicing lifting them every three to four strokes.

Because I didn't understand the need for this and I'm competitive, I thought it best to just try and swim the length of the pool with one breath. I could hear the coach yelling at me to bring my head up and breathe, but I just kicked harder until my hand hit the wall and I threw my head up gasping for air.

Everyone in the entire pool turned toward me as I exhaled loudly and gasped, "I'm okay!"

The coach was still yelling at me, but I was too busy trying to breathe to hear her. Raquel later confessed that she was a former swim team captain from California and didn't want to tell me because she wanted me to learn to swim so we could do the triathlon together. I felt completely bamboozled but her trick did work. Had she told me that she was an expert swimmer, I may have never taken the class. I did learn to swim; I was breathing every three strokes and even flipping at the end of the pool by the end of our three-month session. I moved up in the lanes and my former lane mates improved as well. But I have never felt so out of place.

I always use my bikini analogy for anyone starting something new. We often feel naked and vulnerable showing up and not knowing what to do but the point is we are all novices at anything when we first start. So just show up, strap your goggles on, and get into the pool. The important part is that you are there! You'll eventually learn to breathe and how to draft and even do a flip at the end of the pool if you keep at it.

In the beginning, I really sucked at dating too.

A year after separating with my husband, I felt ready to put myself out there again in the dating pool. The last time I had dated was in college, in the 90's, before cell phones and the internet. Guys would make me their favorite mixtapes to listen to on my Walkman or write me a handwritten letter. Now I was being thrust into an environment that was completely foreign. Long gone were the days of meeting a guy organically, where you'd slowly start to get to know each other, spend some time together, and eventually date if you both liked each other. I don't even think they called it dating anymore in 2010. It was just "hanging out" and "chilling." This was a new day with dating apps, cell phones, and online conversations. I was also juggling being a single mom, running my own business, and navigating the newness of the divorce. I am usually very confident, but suddenly, I was feeling like Bambi on ice, awkward and vulnerable.

I remember how I felt that summer in Spain, years ago. I was just seventeen and I had saved my money to go and stay with Maria, our Spanish exchange student, and her family in Madrid. When I went to my first bar, Maria pulled me aside before I left. She pointed to her eyes with her fingers to indicate I needed to keep my eyes open and said, "Be careful, *Guapa*, you are a light-haired *Americana* and you need to watch out for the *buitres* (vultures)!" By the end of the night, the Spanish boys caught sight and smell of the new meat and started to circle me like a wounded rabbit languishing in an open field. Luckily, Juan, my Spanish neighbor rescued me. He made sure I returned safely to *mi casa*. Possibly I had drunk a few too many *vino tintos* and I tried to kiss him, but he gallantly refused, explaining that we could talk or have a coffee tomorrow. We did eventually get together and had a wonderful romance. Oh, the summer of 1993, but that's another story.

Being awkward and new in dating in a new country at seventeen is something entirely different than re-entering the dating pool at thirty-four with a bunch of baggage and trying to sift through all the candidates who probably are carrying their own baggage too. Where were the Juanillos now? Some said my picker was broken because I was not making the best choices. There was "Terrified Ted," a therapist and ex-drug addict who was too afraid to move forward in a relationship and wanted to keep things "open?" Or what about "The Assassin," appropriately named from his past job experience as a sniper from Mexico who was still doing some sketchy work here in the states. He would pick me up on his shiny black crotch rocket and we would fly across town to go salsa dancing. Can you see me in my hot pink pants, hair blowing in the wind with a smile as big as the Grand Canyon? So much fun, but …dangerous. And he wasn't really the best role model for my kids. Then there was the Croatian Pizza guy, the Polish lifeguard who looked like a young Arnold Schwarzenegger, Crazy in Casablanca, Rude Rudy, Fabio…aka the gypsy/sailor, and Francesco the Favorite. The list goes on…yes, many of them foreigners— I'm a sucker for dark, handsome men with accents. "Mamma Mia!"

When I was quiet and not being tempted by eye-candy, I knew that what I really wanted was to meet someone who would see me. I wanted to be the only woman, not just in the room, but in his world. I longed for a dinner date where I could sit across the table from someone and, although people were moving around us, it would just be background to us. I yearned to have a connection with someone whose eyes weren't shifting around to see a possible prospect or to catch a glimpse of another woman. I prayed for this all the while that I knew I was making a total mess at dating.

Chapter 8:

Your Art Is for Someone

"I can't give them up!" Betsy said. "I just can't sell any of my originals." She was new to painting. Prior to attending Art-Women-Wine classes, she worked with another studio that pushed perfection in pastels. They would work for months on one piece, nitpicking at the details. With that kind of history, I could understand her hesitation to let an original go when it took almost half a year to finally complete it. But my teaching methods are different. I'm a prolific painter and most of my students become prolific, too. Soon their houses are galleries and they become less attached.

"Betsy, I understand that these paintings are very special to you, but in time, when you have so many, you'll realize that you are running out of room. You'll feel better about letting some go. And the good news is that if you make some money by selling them, you'll be able to invest in more canvases and classes so you can continue to paint. Plus, just think about how happy people will be to have your painting. You'll feel happy knowing how much they love the painting and that it's in a good home!"

She held onto those pieces for a long time. Her husband even built her an entire studio with extra storage up top to hold all the originals— and they weren't small, either. These were big paintings— showstoppers to hang over your fireplace. As the paintings kept coming and the storage space became less adequate, she decided to finally sell a few originals. The next thing I heard was that a lady had fallen in love with a couple of her paintings, bought the originals, and hung them in her newly remodeled custom home. A few weeks later, Betsy could show her work in a magazine that had featured that home.

There's a big difference between having your artwork featured in a design magazine and throwing them into storage with mounds of other paintings.

Finally, Betsy felt it. She decided to sell a few other originals. The more she let go, the easier it became and the freer she was to create. To this day, she still sells a ton of prints and other merchandise with her work on it, but if the price is right, she'll sell the original, too.

This is a fear felt by most artists, especially when they start painting. In Art-Women-Wine class, I laugh and assure them that in time, they will allow them to go. Otherwise, their houses will soon look like galleries and their closets will overflow with paintings. Painting is a process that's meant to be shared. I usually keep one favorite painting from every series of work that I've done. It doesn't have to be the biggest or even strongest painting, but if there is something that really connects with me, I'll keep it.

All the others are meant for someone else. If you don't release your work as you go, it can kill your creativity. I tell my students, "You don't own your art. The pieces you create are on loan to you from God. You get to enjoy that painting for a little while, helping it to grow and become something wonderful, just like a foster parent would. In the end, however, the painting must find its 'forever home' and the place it was always meant to live."

How selfish we would be to keep a painting that wasn't designed for us. If you knew that something you made could make someone else so happy, but instead you held onto it and stuffed it into your closet, wouldn't that be a terrible thing? There's a story in the Bible about a master who gives each of his servants a certain amount of money. Two of the servants go out and invest the money and bring back more than what the master had given them, but one of the servants buries the money and brings back only what the master had given him. The master gets angry with that servant and casts him out.

There are many different beliefs about what that parable means, but I understand it to mean that God gives us talents and he expects us to use them and share them. If you are burying your talents, I would strongly suggest that you get a shovel and start digging. Those talents are on loan from God, and he's expecting you to do something with them. When you grasp the idea that you are just fostering a painting, it opens a path to letting those paintings go.

When I first created my website, my then-husband argued that some of my pieces were old and shouldn't be added to the site. We had a little disagreement about it because, although the paintings were older, they were still strong pieces, and they were still for sale. I thought that they should be included on the site. I won.

Not long after the site went up, I got a message from my husband's cousin who fell in love with one of my pieces. It was an earlier work—one that I had done in college. I had used oil pastels, which I had hardly used since. She contacted us and said, "I want this painting and I don't even care how much it costs because it's supposed to be mine." She bought it immediately and I shipped it to Arkansas to its new home. What happened next is the incredible part. After she bought the first one, she and her husband flew up to visit us and to see all my other paintings. After looking through my work, they bought three more for their new home. These were big, expensive paintings that really helped our family financially. We would have totally missed out on those sales if we hadn't put the smaller pastel painting online.

Selling my work was rewarding but what I loved most was how much she connected to that painting. She made it her screen saver and she placed it in a very private and special place. She said, "Don't tell me about the meaning behind the painting because it means something very important to me and I just want to keep that meaning sacred." Realizing that something I had painted meant so much to her and that I helped to bring such happiness to her just by sharing my work made me feel fulfilled. The connection that she had with my paintings was so strong, she ended up being an ardent collector of my artwork.

Probably my very favorite story about a painting finding its right home and owner is the history of a painting entitled *Time*. It was Christmastime, and I had taught a private workshop at a woman's house in Lake Oswego, which I nicknamed "Lake Ego" because of its snooty and uppity vibe. The house was modern with concrete floors and floor-to-ceiling windows. It was cold, ostentatious, and felt a little like a New York gallery without the paintings.

When the workshop ended and I was getting ready to leave, the owner, Karen, asked me about art placement and my opinion on a giant wall in her foyer. The wall was the first thing you saw when you walked in, and it was the best placement for a focal painting. She added that she was very concerned about money, which was hard for me to believe, looking around her place.

I said, "With a strong piece on that wall acting as an anchor for the eye, you could get away with Target knockoffs and not-so-original IKEA prints in other places."

She asked, "Could you create something for that space?"

"Absolutely," I replied. "When would you need it?"

"Well, my Christmas party and open house is in two weeks. I want to make a statement. Is there any way you could get it done in two weeks?"

That was a big ask. I knew that this space couldn't be filled by any of my past work; it would have to be custom designed. Christmas was right around the corner. It would take me sacrificing and putting everything else on hold to complete it. A project of this magnitude would be a stretch for me as an artist, but if I did it right, it could be brilliant. Furthermore, it would really help a struggling artist at Christmastime.

I said, "Yes, I can do it!"

I gave her the options for canvas sizes, and we made an agreement that she would pay for the materials, and I would create the piece. Upon delivery, she could pay upfront, in installments, and I even offered a trade in services—her husband was a lawyer, and I needed some advice for my business. If she decided she didn't love the piece after the Christmas party, then I would take the piece back and apply the money she spent on the materials as a rental fee to have the painting at the party and through the holidays. It all seemed fair and agreeable.

Now, I just needed to get the materials and create a six-foot-by-six-foot masterpiece in two weeks. *No problem!* She gave me the name of her husband's company, which I thought would be cool to incorporate into the painting to make it more personalized. It was the biggest painting I had ever done. I wasn't even sure how I was going to do it, but I had a deadline and three very sweet little kids who needed Santa to visit this year, so that motivated me to make it happen.

The piece came together like a symphony where every note hangs on the other in a perfect compilation of harmonies. It seemed effortless and it was beautiful. Finally, I placed the name of his company, TIME, in the bottom right corner and signed my name. It truly was my best work.

After seeing it, my grandpa commented that I had just entered a new realm as an artist. Even my stubborn, detailed, and critical professor grandpa loved this piece. It was perfect!

The night before taking it to the owner, however, I woke up in a hot sweat. I sat straight up and woke up my hubby in bed.

"Holy cow! The name of his company was *THINK,* not *TIME!*" I slapped my forehead. "Honey, what am I going to do?"

You might think it's easy for artists to just change things in their paintings, and sometimes it is. But there are times when you know deep down in your gut that the piece is right the way it is and if you go back to change anything—if you swap a word, add a color, anything—the piece would lose its greatness. I went downstairs and looked at it. It looked like it should have the word TIME in it. It was meant to be. That piece was done and for me to change it would be disastrous.

Now I had to think of the reason why I added the word "TIME" so I could explain this to my client. They had to believe and know that the piece was meant to be called *TIME.* Delivery day arrived and the painting was so big, I had to use our trailer to drop the painting off. Karen was thrilled. When she asked why I added the word "TIME," I invented something about how precious and important time is. I dropped off the contract, and she assured me that they would return the signed contract and payment after the Christmas party and open house.

I was invited to the open house and Christmas party, and it was a great success. Women who worked out all day praised my work with Botoxed lips and clinked their wine glasses with mine with their manicured fingernails. Men in tailored suits sipping on bourbon, whiskey—or whatever ritzy, successful, golf-playing men sip—made nice remarks and acted interested in my process. I was accepted like a servant girl being called into the parlor to be praised for delivering her mistress's baby.

"Nice job!"

"Oh, you are very talented!"

"Do you do this for a living?"

"Aren't you gifted!"

And then there was the implied, "Now, run along."

Still, I held my head high and acted confident like I had learned from Grandma Dottie. Perhaps the best compliment I received that evening was from a woman who apparently had too much bubbly: "That painting is *so* sexy. I just want to get naked and rub my body all over it!" The painting really was a showstopper; it was the belle of the ball, and with all the positive feedback,

I was certain that the owner and her husband would also love it. Within a few days of the party, however, I received an email from her husband: "We reject all of your offers, A, B, and C."

> *What? How?* I felt like a giant fist punched me in the gut. I saw all the Christmas gifts I hoped to buy for the kids disappear from under the tree. I felt sick.

He continued: "We will not be giving you the painting back until you pay us back for the materials fee." Where was Karen? Did she not tell him of our agreement and the fact that she begged me to do this last minute? Did he not hear the rave reviews from his hoity-toity neighbors? It had earned its rent. I was in a panic because I was up against a lawyer, and I had so little leverage. I didn't have any signed documents, just a verbal agreement from Karen. I called him immediately. I stayed calm and tried to reason with him, explaining the agreement that Karen and I had made and how wrong it was for him to keep the painting. I asked what he thought was a fair amount to pay for it. In the end, he wouldn't offer me anything, but he finally agreed to allow me to retrieve the painting.

I'll never forget the day we drove over there. Grandma Dottie came with me, and she was furious. It was snowing and the roads were bad, but Christmas or no Christmas, I needed to get this painting while he was still in agreement for me to do so. We arrived at the oversized, cold, lifeless house. The cement floors reflected the freezing feeling I had when we opened the door. Karen was nowhere to be seen, but her conniving lawyer husband was there. He opened the door with a veneer smile and waved us in. There was my painting, leaning against the wall like the last kid waiting to be reluctantly called to join the team at recess.

It was sad. I had no use for a painting that I had created for them, for this space. What was I going to do with a giant painting of this magnitude? We didn't even have a wall big enough to hold it, but I would be damned rather than let them steal this piece from me. So we loaded the painting, said a few parting words, and slowly drove home through the snow.

That Christmas was tight. We were planning on that money and now we had very little. The kids were happy and grateful for the little gifts we were able to get them, but inside I was grieving. I found a home for *TIME* in our office for the time being, and every time I saw it I felt a little pang of sorrow in my gut.

By March, spring was showing off. The pain of the rejected Christmas painting had long passed, and I moved on with painting, running my husband's business, and life in general. Years prior, I had handed my business card to a developer and mentioned that if he ever needed art for any of his buildings or businesses, I was his gal! This kind man remembered me and gave me a call. He had developed several buildings in town and was curious if I would be open to doing some art consultation. We agreed to meet, and he started walking me through the building and walls that could potentially add art.

We were on the tail end of the tour, and he came to this unusual space in the foyer. There used to be an opening in the brick, but then they had to add a wall there, which looked odd. It needed a big piece of artwork to look purposeful or possibly a mural—something that might tie it in with the space.

As we concluded the tour, I asked him about his values, understanding that these can dictate or influence the type of artwork he would love. I said, "Wes, what's the most important thing in your life?"

He replied, "Time."

I heard the angels sing!

"Excuse me, could you please tell me again? What is the most important thing in your life?"

And he said, "Time. Time is the most important thing in my life, Elida."

"Well, I think I have a painting for you." Within the next few weeks, *TIME* found her permanent home, and I received the full price without any complaints, negotiations, or trouble. Furthermore, this was the start of a wonderful working relationship. I brought in several more pieces for the building and was even commissioned to do a giant installation that is a highlight for the building.

My time as a foster parent to my painting was over. It had all the drama that a messy adoption can have. But, reflecting, I realize that the real parent hadn't arrived yet. Now, whenever I have a painting that doesn't sell or is overlooked and undervalued, I know that he or she is journeying my way, looking for my piece.

Just like your paintings, you are meant for someone too.

In Florence, every street is a museum. "Over there is where Dante first saw Beatrice at the church. That old house on the corner is where Galileo used to live." The cobblestone streets, the museums, the Ponte Vecchio bridge with its dreamlike gold shops lining its walls. Florence is flourishing with art and history. It's also known for its leather craftsmanship. The Florentines have a secret skill that, so far, remains inimitable. The Chinese, like most everywhere, have moved in to take over much of the textile business, making good copies of Italian clothing designs. But they hadn't been able to break the code on how Tuscans do their leather. Nobody has. Top secret.

That day, I was leading the pack as we ventured into the markets. Fr. Gio, who has no need for shopping or leather goods, positioned himself on a corner near San Lorenzo square to sketch. The rest of us were unleashed on the streets to discover some of the best clothes, shoes, handbags and leather goods in the world. I turned down a side street just off the main markets when I saw it.

It was as if a light from heaven came down and landed on a red leather jacket. There were scalloped sleeves and a pleated bodice. The details on the collar showed the craftsmanship of a real artist who clearly knew design. Everything was hand-stitched to perfection. The magnetic attraction pulled us together with a snap. I started ripping it off the manikin. Just as I was getting the buttons undone, I heard a deep, buttery, rich voice say, "*Buongiorno Bella.* How can I help you?" I felt another magnetic pull and turned to see a man with a smile that was just as beautiful as his voice.

"*Bongiorno*," I replied, "and who are you?" He laughed and tilted his head as he reached in to kiss my left and right cheeks (the customary greeting in Italy).

"I'm Sam. I work here at the shop, and I would love to help you with that jacket." Before long we were all piling in like a bunch of chickens trying to get into the henhouse before the sun sets. We were plucking things off the racks and trying things on. Eventually, some of the group left for other stores and the rest of the group found their way to the couch in the back of the shop and snuggled in to *ooh* and *ahh* for the things I tried on. Wine appeared. I didn't know that trying on jackets was such an event, but that day, the small crowd acted like I was trying on my wedding dress. I was front and center and Sam was dressing me. As he pulled the jacket around me and buttoned the front buttons, I got a whiff of his cologne— not too strong, just enough, and then that smile again. Gah!

"I kind of like you getting me dressed," I quipped. He smiled a little brighter, pulled me in a little tighter as he buttoned the front buttons and retorted, "I could get you dressed every morning if you'd like." The women all tittered from the couch, clearly enjoying the flirtation. I was having a hard time remembering that I was there for the jacket. This felt like something more. Then came a scarf. Some accessories. He shouted out in Italian and a few other guys appeared, all attending to us, as we continued this ritualistic process of trying on a stand-out leather jacket.

The sleeves were a little long. He showed me how they would alter it to make it fit perfectly. Then, he stepped back, smiled, and said, "This jacket is made for you!" I was already flustered with his voice, the cologne, and the heady sensation of being so close to this alluring man that I couldn't think straight. I took a deep breath and realized that he was right, the jacket was perfect. I started to pull out my billfold when …reality check. *Wait! I'm on a strict budget.*

I asked, "How much is it? Sorry, but I'm a single mom with three kids and a mortgage." He grabbed the calculator and showed me the conversion in dollars.

Then replied, "I'm a single dad with a daughter and a mortgage too. No wife."

He caught my eye meaningfully. The coat was too much for my budget. Reluctantly, I started to unwind the scarf and slip off the jacket. Before leaving, though, I reached into my pocket and handed him my business card. "If the jacket goes on sale or you want to take me out for dinner, here's my card." I asked for a pen. Then, I wrote *RED JACKET* on the card, "so you'll remember me."

He replied, "Oh, I will remember you. You don't have to write anything on that card."

There was a lot of cackling from the hen house and reminders: "Don't call her. Text her instead," because of the foreign fees for cell phones. After a lot of commotion, I was able to round up the chickens and drive them out the door to continue our shopping excursion.

Later that day, I got a text from Sam and an offer for dinner. I decided to hang with the group for a bit at our group dinner and then head out to meet him. Sandy, one of my original Art-Women-Wine ladies, pulled me aside to remind me, "You can't be serious with this guy. He only works at a leather shop, but don't you come home without that jacket!"

There was more well-meaning, unsolicited advice: "Don't get into his car. He might kidnap you."

"Watch your drink at all times, you could get roofied."

"Keep your phone on at all times!" And so on.

On my way over to meet him, I got lost. I couldn't see any street signs. Who knew they were on the sides of the buildings about ten feet up?

I reluctantly called him to explain my lateness. "I'm sorry but I'm lost."

He reassured me and then gently asked me to describe what I could see around me. After a few explanations, he said, "Stay where you are. I'll find you."

Then, there he was, like the leading man in a movie, walking towards me as it began to rain. He was wearing a suit and slid open an umbrella as he approached, his smile as big as I had remembered and his voice deep and soothing. I slipped my arm into his as we started to walk. It all felt so familiar, a Deja vu moment— like we had known each other for a long time.

We walked across the city to the leather shop where a slick black BMW was parked. As I slid into the passenger side, I heard the warnings from the women in my head, "Don't get into his car. You could be kidnapped!" He climbed in on the other side.

He started the car and then said, "Wait here for a moment. I need to take care of something really quick." He ran across the plaza and embraced a young man who was with a group of other Italians. Everything seemed amicable, like he was seeing an old friend. He pulled out a wad of money from his pocket and placed it in the hand of the guy and then ran back to the car. "*Andiamo Bella*, now to our dinner plans," and he pulled out of the plaza.

My mind began to race, why did he give that money to that guy? My eyes scanned the car's dashboard and noticed a picture. As I looked closer, I saw that it was Marlon Brando from *The Godfather* movie. Just below it I saw a cigar.

Dear God, Elida, this guy is a mafioso! I could feel my breathing speeding up.

I began the interrogation. "Who was that guy you were giving money to in the plaza?"

"How can you afford this fancy car when you just work at a leather shop?"

"Why do you have a picture of the Vito Corleone?" I kept on. He good-naturedly answered each of them.

"Darling, the guy I gave money to is my nephew, Marco."

"I own that leather shop. I also own the leather bag shop across the way as well and one more shop in the market."

When I asked the third question, his concern grew until he pulled off the road and stopped. He turned and opened his arm toward me to lean it on the back of my seat and asked, "Elida, what is wrong? What's happening with you right now?"

Much too honestly, I burst out, "I am not supposed to get into the car with you. I don't know you and, for all I know, you could be a mass murderer! You have this picture of *The Godfather* so you could be part of the mafia. I mean, who knows? You might be planning to roofie my drink later so you can drug me to take me some place and rape me and kill me and then throw my body in a ditch somewhere!" By this time, the pressure and my fear was overwhelming and I put my hands over my face.

He took a big breath and then rested his hand on my shoulder. "*Principessa,* I can explain everything. The picture of *The Godfather* was a local promotion, a renewal of the movie that someone just handed me. The cigar, well I like cigars. I explained to you about Marco, my nephew, and the car, but what is this thing about a roofie, or drug put into your drink? I haven't ever even heard of such a thing. Do they do that in your country?"

He continued, "I only wanted to bring you to this restaurant because it's special and, if I only have one night with you, then I want to make sure it's the best I can offer. But I can take you back into the city if you'd feel more comfortable. I just want to do something nice for you." I took a deep breath and after a little more conversation and some more assurance we continued on our way.

When we arrived, I noticed the curved architecture was like a cave. One wall was full of wine barrels with an actual cave behind it. The tables were round with white tablecloths and fresh flowers on each table. The flicker of candles was its only light. At first, they tried to seat us at the front but Sam insisted we be placed at the best table in the back. In short, the ambience was exactly how you'd imagine a romantic Italian restaurant to look like. He started with an order of prosecco and then clasped his hands together and leaned across the table towards me, "*Allora, Principessa*, tell me what kind of food you'd like to eat."

I said, "Sam, this is your special place. I prefer you order whatever you think I would like, and I'll be happy with whatever you choose."

He leaned back into his chair, his smile widened. "Really, you are okay with me ordering everything. Then, be prepared to really enjoy it." He motioned to the waiter to come to the table.

The night unfolded slowly, like a rose when it carefully breaks out of a bud into full bloom. The wine kept coming. The food arrived in their proper courses. For hours, we ate, drank, and talked until there was no more room in our stomachs and no more words to share.

At some point, the powerful realization came: *This was what I have longed for. This moment in time was the very thing I had prayed for.* Here was this handsome man, in a beautiful country taking me to dinner. Even though the restaurant was full of attractive women, they were outside the world of him and me. Even with my mini meltdown in the car where I almost missed this opportunity, he was able to give me the reassurance I needed. I was smitten and I didn't think the night could get any better.

Afterwards he drove us to the top of the city to Piazzale Michelangelo. He put his jacket around my shoulders, and we walked around to the front of his car. Florence is gorgeous by day but by night it's spectacular! We took in the city lights, smoking cigars. Then we laid back on the hood of his car and kissed as we watched for shooting stars. We stayed there until the sun peeked over the hills. On our way back down, we stopped at his leather shop. It was early, maybe 6 am, and he opened the sliding door. In the back of the shop was a man, smoking a cigarette, and cutting strips of leather. He looked up over his reading glasses, and shouted out of the side of his mouth, "*Sammy, como estai?*" It was the designer, working on a few pieces before the morning crowd arrived. His drawings and tools were spread out across the table, and it was the most beautiful site I had ever seen until my eyes crossed the room, and I saw the red leather jacket again.

Sam followed my gaze and then walked over to the jacket and pulled it off the hanger. "I want you to have it," he said, slipping it onto my shoulders. The cigarette almost drop from the designer's mouth. Sam continued, "You didn't have time to do the shopping you needed because you were with me. As a token of our friendship, pick out some gifts for your family." I tried to argue, but he wouldn't have it. He walked over and opened the other shop too. So, for the next few hours I had a personal shopping experience at both the leather coat shop and his leather bag shop where I loaded up with gifts for my entire family. He was so generous. I couldn't even fathom that someone would want to do all of this for me. I was overwhelmed.

That night will forever be remembered as one of my favorite nights. Sam reminded me that I am not for everyone, nor just anyone. I am treasured. A gift. After experiencing a long line of not-so-great dates, he was the first who made me feel like an orphan who had found her home. The dinner, the evening, the red jacket and all of the leather goods were gifts, but the biggest gift was his complete attention and care. To have someone who only has eyes for you, who sees you, loves you and asks for nothing in return was the best and most pure gift I could ever ask for. I thought our little fling would be just for one night, and with that, I was truly satisfied. But Florence is like one of those music boxes. It's beautiful at first glance, but then it opens and surprises you with a dance and a sweet melody that goes on and on.

Chapter 9:

It's for the Greater Good of the Painting

Kerri is one of those women that you love to hate. Not like hate-hate but in a I-hate-you-because-you-are-so-beautiful kind of way. She's one of those artists who is good at everything, and I mean everything! You hate her just a little more because she doesn't even realize how good she is. She can garden, bake, cook, decorate, and paint. Her background is design so, to add to her giftedness, she's added training and experience which produces exquisite ideas on colors, composition, and shading.

Like most human beings, however, she has her kryptonite. Her kryptonite is *perfectionism.* She becomes fixated on a painting and is so intent on perfection, not missing one detail, that she loses herself in the piece and, in the end, she loses the painting too. Some artists would love to become more focused on details but not Kerri. She longs to be set free from her constraints—to have more flow and looser strokes. She is constantly fighting her tendency to make things exact and really desires a more relaxed and abstract style.

Recently, Kerri was painting a barn. She was off to a good start, but despite her promise that she wasn't going to mess with it until the next class, she did homework (another reason we hate her) and showed up with the painting almost finished. The problem was that the piece had an uneasiness about it. It seemed to be fighting with itself. There was the barn and many other detailed depictions in the background.

I asked her, "Which of these items do you want to be the star of the show?"

She replied, "The barn."

"Well, then, for the greater good of the painting, you've got to get rid of all this other stuff because it's taking away from your star! The sky needs to be painted over, the grass needs to be washed over in a more consistent color, and…" I began painting over the grass with a washed-out dark green, getting rid of many of the meticulous details that had taken her hours to paint. Within seconds, poof! They were gone forever. Kerri sighed and reluctantly took the big brush back. As happy as she was to find the solution, I could see the sadness in her eyes as she faced the prospect of painting over hours of work. In the end, she discovered that it was the right move. The final product was stunning.

I once began a mixed media painting by carefully selecting all sorts of things I love from magazines, books, and bins of collage papers. After I glued all the images down onto a big wooden canvas, I realized that the piece was too busy. My original plan was to add glaze to the images to get them to show through, not disappear. It wasn't coming together, however, no matter how long I kept working on it. The images weren't emanating the atmosphere I wanted. Instead, they were fighting with one another and bogging down the entire piece.

I stepped back to get some perspective. Although there were so many of the images that I loved, I noticed that a little black-and-white picture of a cowboy kept grabbing my attention. What if I painted over all the other images and just kept the cowboy? The thought made my stomach twinge. Why would I wipe out all the images that I absolutely loved for just this one image? I tried again to keep them all but to no avail. My eyes kept pointing me in the direction of painting over everything except the cowboy.

I finally did it, though I felt terrible during the process. As I was painting, I repeated, "It's for the greater good of the painting." When I was finished, my heart pounded as I stepped back to look at the damage. But I was pleasantly surprised. All the images added texture and depth to the painting, but the little cowboy was able to shine through without distractions. There he stood, the star of the show! This bold act saved the piece. Had I tried to keep all the images visible, it would not have been as strong and stunning as it is.

I called it *Urban Cowboy* and it hangs proudly over my parents' bed in their master bedroom. It gives me so much joy to know that they love it. I also feel a sense of happiness knowing that even though you don't see all the other images, they are still there supporting the star of the show. The painting wouldn't be the same without all those images texturing the background. Sometimes we must let go of things, even the things that we love, for the greater good of the painting.

Sometimes we must let go of things, even the things (and people) we love, for the greater good in our lives.

Sam's and my romance blossomed. We skyped each other regularly after that first trip to Italy and often talked about plans to see each other. In early November, he explained that he couldn't come to see me because of a situation with his daughter. I was disappointed but I understood. Both Sam and I respected each other's obligations as parents and understood that our romance and love was second priority.

Later, he brought up another option. "Darling, you never really got a chance to come to visit Venice. What if, for our second date, I show you *Venezia*?" I leaned toward the computer screen and tilted my head to make sure I heard correctly, "You want to fly me to Italy and show me Venice?" He smiled and nodded his head in agreement. I sat back, held my finger up exaggeratedly to say *Hold on a minute* and then pretended to check my calendar. Instead, I walked into the kitchen and did a little happy dance!

I mean seriously, I had been dating "loservilles" who won't even call me for a second date and this guy is flying me back to Italy? Can I pinch myself now? I took some big breaths and then casually strolled back into the office to finish our talk.

"It looks like I'm free that month but if I come, I'll need to do some scouting for my next Italy tour. He reassured me that we could schedule whatever time I needed for work.

And the next thing I knew, I was on a plane to Italy…again!

He picked me up in Florence and we jumped on the train to Venice. The ride went by quickly because we had so much to talk about. It all felt natural and easy, just like the first night we met. Everything about Sam was such a breath of fresh air from what I had been dealing with. When we arrived in Venice, it was like a romantic movie scene. The fog was rolling in and the crisp air swept across the gray cobblestone streets. Mist hovered over the canals, swirling around the boats and through the crowds. People were buttoning up their long woolen sailor coats with big brass buttons and then wrapping their scarves around their starchy collars. It was magical.

Sam had already set the bar so high for me with that dinner in Florence that I distanced myself from it. It seemed unrealistic to expect the royal treatment to continue, especially since we were going to be together for several days. Plus, I remembered, *The flight to Italy already far exceeded my expectations for a second date.*

But when we arrived at the hotel, I realized how absurd my precautions were. Our room opened to a balcony overlooking St. Mark's Square. The hotel was built in the classic Venetian Gothic style with lancet arches and the interior revealed its Byzantine and Ottoman influences. Colorful fabrics draped around massive marble pillars, billowing from the ceilings and tumbling to the marble floors. Tight, winding stairs led to multiple levels, each one with some exciting mystery. The marble-lined bathroom showcased a big soaker bathtub with a window overlooking the water. I was like a kid in a candy shop, wanting to see and touch everything.

As I sank down into the bubbles, I felt like a movie star. On my first tour to Italy, I imagined I was Julia Roberts in *Eat, Pray, Love.* I was searching for answers and exploring the simple beauties of life after a difficult divorce. Now, I imagined I was Julia Roberts in *Pretty Woman* — not in a working girl kind of way, ha-ha!

but in the I'm-living-way-above-my-pay-grade-luxury-life kind of way. As I slipped into my white, terry cloth robe and slippers, the transportation was complete. *Calgon, take me away!*

That evening, we strolled through the streets, ate delicious food, and topped it off with a romantic gondola ride down the canals—kissing under the bridges and musing over the reflections on the water from all the colored lights. It blew away my expectations and exceeded my dreams. The next morning, Sam suggested that we do a slow morning so I could recover from my trip, and order in room service for breakfast. I scrolled the menu, and everything looked so delicious that I couldn't decide. Sheepishly, I asked if I could order one of everything. His smile widened. He always seemed to get so much joy out of my childlike behavior and nodded approvingly as he kissed my forehead. Soon, the knock on the door came and my eyes widened when the waiter rolled in a table with a white linen tablecloth and each item was served on silver trays with silver plate covers. The table was completely full. It was like Christmas. I opened a plate cover and *Surprise!* A new fabulous Italian delicacy to enjoy. We sat out on the balcony, drinking our cappuccinos and eating copious amounts of food all morning long as we watched the boats and gondolas wind their ways through the canals. I was in heaven.

Later, drinks at the bar where Hemingway wrote, walks along the canals, romantic kisses in the alleyways, a day trip to Murano where Sam almost bought me a giant blown glass chandelier (which I had no use for as I didn't even own a house)! It was all so luxurious, so healing, and so lovely. After our time in Venice, Sam made good on his promise to help me do some "recon" for my upcoming tours. We visited a farm or *Agritourismo* in Siena, checked out some hotels and places to stay in Tuscany, and explored some sites in Florence as well. When the trip came to an end, I felt sad about leaving, but I reminded myself that it was just the beginning of something wonderful.

A few months later, he came to visit me in the US. We road-tripped to San Francisco over the holidays where he met my grandparents and spent time with my extended family. You learn a lot about a person when you travel together, and it seemed that almost everything we did together was effortless and easy. We communicated well and found that we were a great team. There were so many cliches that seemed to describe what I was experiencing. As my mom used to say, "They got along like peas and carrots." Others would say, "They are a match made in heaven," and I agreed. We seemed perfect for one another. I was falling in love with this man, a gift from God in my broken life.

I teamed up with Fr. Gio to organize our next Italian expedition to the Amalfi Coast that spring. I planned to come about a week early so I could see Sam in Florence before heading south to Sorrento. When I arrived, he announced he had a surprise and all I needed was my bathing suit, a few dresses and sandals. I must admit I wasn't happy to be leaving since I had just arrived, but my love of adventure helped me to put my game face on. I threw my stuff in a backpack and off we went to the airport. As we walked to the gate, I noticed that people didn't look Italian. They dressed in different styles and were speaking a different language. My eyes scanned over the crowd to the gate we were boarding and that is where I saw the words, *Marrakech, Morocco.*

When we walked out of the airport we were transported into the chaotic energy of another culture—camels and donkeys walking along the street and turbaned men appearing out of nowhere, shoving a cobra or a monkey in my face. The brilliant colors are overwhelming and the main square changes out three times a day. In the morning, it's full of fruits and veggies, then textiles and food for lunch, and in the evening, new items for sale as well as dinner food and entertainment.

I had seen sights like these in movies like *Indiana Jones, Casablanca,* or *Aladdin,* but they cannot fully bring you into the heat, the noise, the smells, and the vitality. The men squat down around a kettle, sipping tea, and chirping in their native language. And seven times a day, the loud horn blasts to call the faithful to prayer was a constant reminder that we were indeed not in the USA, or even Europe, anymore. I was still reeling from the fact that I was in Africa and not in Italy when we arrived at our hotel. My senses were overloaded. There was a giant brown stucco wall around the entire property and on each side a huge garden gate with ornate black iron designs all around its massive wooden structure. The gate was huge and heavy, with a small call button next to it. Sam buzzed it and the gate opened slowly, then as soon as we stepped in, we were transformed into another world. Everything was quiet, pristine and manicured. The energy immediately shifted from chaos to calm, and I let out a huge sigh. After all the stimulation, I needed this. The hotel was called the Red Door, properly named for its red door as its main entrance. There were only eight rooms, but they were large and spacious, each one with a balcony that overlooked the garden and pool. The pool had a little island in the middle with palm trees. I soon learned that while laying by the pool, one could get anything they desired with just a wave of your hand. It was way too bougie for this simple, rural girl, but it was an easy adjustment. I mean, who's going to turn down freshly squeezed orange juice or a mint julep on a hot day?

The vacation unfolded nicely with just the right amount of sightseeing, eating, drinking, dancing and plenty of time for rest and relaxing back at the Red Door. On our last night we went to a special dinner show where there were live performances of belly dancers and fire blowers. The live music was going, drinks were flowing, and Sam pulled me close and whispered in my ear, "I love you." I demurely smiled and we embraced. Then, he slid a small black leather box into my hand. I looked down and saw it had a gold symbol of the Ponte Vecchio, the famous bridge in Florence renowned for its specialized jewelry. When I opened it, I saw an intricate diamond ring, designed like the shape of the Ponte Vecchio itself. It was so spectacular and shiny— just like him. A bright light in my life. I was flabbergasted and didn't know what to say. He explained that he had never been married before, even though he had a long-time partnership with his daughter's mom. He never felt the need to marry, but now, he did. He wanted to marry me.

I was speechless. I tried to explain that even though I loved him and would love to marry him, I wasn't ready. There were too many unfinished things in my life and too many unknowns in our lives ahead. He slid the ring on my finger and noticed it was too big, so moved it over to the middle finger. Without hesitation he said, "*Princepessa*, wear it on the middle finger as a reminder of our friendship and love and if you ever decide you'll marry me, we can get it sized down for you to wear it on your ring finger." Then he reached in and kissed me again ever so softly on the side of my cheek. If anyone could write a book on the right thing to say to women, it would be Sam. How could I resist such an offer? So, I accepted his ring and treasured his words.

That summer, I decided to take my kids and niece to live in Florence for the summer. Secretly, I desired to move there and wanted to see how they would handle living in another country. Each day, Sam would ask us about our plans and give us money to make it happen. The kids always had money for gelato runs, museums or to hang out at "the internet cafe" where they had Wi-Fi. My daughter, Emily and my niece, Elsa, both fourteen, became terrors on their bikes, flying down the cobblestone streets and markets. The guys at the market booths didn't even bother to yell out, "Bella, I have the perfect scarf for you. You would look *bellissima*," because they saw them as locals.

I took all the kids to Rome in August in 100-degree weather where I marched them all over the city, so they could see it all in a day. Not a good idea. There were many tears and frustrations on both ends. Later, they appropriately named it "the death march of Rome." We climbed the Duomo in Florence, visited Venice, and traveled to Cagli, the little town I love so much in the La Marche region. Then we headed South to Lecce in Puglia (the heel of the boot) where my kids were easily spotted on the beach because the boys had board shorts (not speedos) and the girls were wearing their tops. We connected with Sam's extended family for a special night. Sometime during dinner, I realized that the entire meal had come from within one mile of their home. The fish came from the sea and had been caught in nets with the help of my boy. The veggies, fruit, olives and wine came from the garden or the fields around us. I leaned over the table and whispered to my kids, "Remember this night because you may never have a meal like this again!" It was a magical time and forever will be locked in my heart as one of my favorite meals.

There were also some hard and unexpected things too. Italy is a fabulous place to visit but not as easy to live in. Life with no Costco or car to load groceries was tough. Also, I found that doing laundry with no dryer for seven people was a lot harder. I remember Emily coming in to drop off her jeans. I took a quick sniff and handed them back with a bottle of Febreeze. Unless those jeans were walking into the laundry on their own, she should keep wearing them. My niece, a prolific tennis player, could not find a place to play tennis without paying huge fees to private clubs. Things we take for granted in the Pacific Northwest like free parks and courts were virtually non-existent in Italy. Also, no baseball parks and fields for the boys to play. Yes, there were a few soccer fields that you could schedule a practice on if you were part of a league, but baseball fields were few and far between and baseball was a huge part of the boys' lives at that time. The three months in Italy allowed me to see a different perspective.

Usually, it is so romanticized. The glow and aura were wearing off.

Still, Sam continued wooing me in between kids, work and life. We'd go out for date nights. There was that one night he took me to a special restaurant, and they brought me out a dessert that literally had fireworks exploding from it. It wasn't even my birthday. Or the other time we went to a "silence dance club" where everyone had to wear headphones to hear the music as we danced outside overlooking the city of Florence. He knew that I loved surprises, variety, and adventure and he always delivered.

The summer was coming to an end, and I was feeling this looming sadness as I knew I would need to go back home soon. I was feeling torn between the man I loved and the life I had back in the United States. I knew in my heart that we couldn't continue the transatlantic journey every few months to see each other. Something had to give. I also knew deep down that as much as I wished we could all just move to Italy; it became clear that living in another country would not be feasible for us. Sam and I discussed possibly moving to New York City. I could further my art career and it would be closer to Italy so he could continue working with his leather shops. We'd both be a six-hour flight from our families. It seemed like a good compromise. We began taking steps toward this possibility, dreaming about a new life together with our kids in NYC.

And then I got a terrible feeling in my gut. I knew what I was supposed to do, but I didn't want to do it. As Christians, we talk about the prompting of the Holy Spirit. It's that gut instinct that tells you clearly, without any confusion, the next step and despite what you think you want, you KNOW what you must do. I imagined uprooting my kids from Washington and moving them across the United States. I had done it once before when I separated from my ex-husband and moved from Texas to my childhood home in Washington. I remembered how difficult the move was, but I'd had the support of my family, so that smoothed the transition. Ten years later, I was looking at moving again—but this time away from my family. My parents had become very involved with my kids. My sister, who is also my best friend, lived just three hours away, and my little brother was also in the area. My cousins and nearly all my other relatives were on the west coast. Also, my children's father lived there and, as much as I disliked him, I knew that having him involved in their lives was still important.

Then I thought about Sam. Sam's daughter was very close to Sam's sisters in Florence. His mom visited from Ethiopia for six months at a time. Sam's daughter had lost her mom just a year before and I knew how important this extended family having—especially the female influences—would be for her. She also spent time with her grandparents in Belgium and it was an easy flight to visit them in the summers from Italy. What would her life be like in America, in a country and culture she didn't know, and with no extended family whom she felt comfortable with? I realized that "for the greater good of the painting," I would need to let Sam go. I would need to paint over all my favorite parts, for the greater good of this painting.

It broke my heart; it broke his heart. Our priority was to our kids, and maybe that was the thing we loved most about each other. We chose what was right for them over our feelings. A sacrifice of love for the greater good. As I got onto the plane, leaving Italy and Sam, I felt like Grace Kelly from that scene in Casablanca. She glanced back at the man she loved and chose what was right over what she felt. Gah, choosing what's right sometimes really sucks! And for the first time in my life, I left a man not because of his lies or bad behavior but because we chose what was best for our families. The lessons and healing weren't lost, those beautiful memories are always there, buried deep into my heart. They are all the layers of the painting that give it the texture and depth to make a masterpiece. I will forever be grateful. The music box to my heart had been opened and now this little ballerina started to dance.

Chapter 10:

Don't Use the C-Word

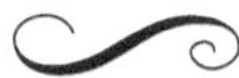

I was teaching an artist-in-residence program to a group of second graders, and everyone was happily busy drawing butterflies with pastels. I looked around and noticed that at one table, Lucy had added some polka dots to her butterfly. Her project appeared cute and clean and altogether perfect. Lucy struck me as the kind of girl who usually follows rules. She would probably want to make her butterfly look like a real butterfly or something that would be clean and perfect, too. She strategically put her dots in places where a real butterfly might have dots and she daintily started to complete her background color by staying within the lines. I noticed she was copying the same color format that I used, and she was making a close rendition of my sample piece.

At the other end of the table sat Sadie. She was engrossed in the process of blending her colors and doing a brilliant job of mixing the brightest, contrasting colors. Her sweatshirt sleeves were pushed up and her bare arms were covered in a vibrant pink. One look at Sadie's face, with pastels smeared across it, and I could make an educated guess about what her project looked like. I walked around to see if I was right. *Yep*. The outside lines were blurred into the background. I could feel the movement, the passion, and the energy pulsing through the drawing. It was beautiful to see how the spirit of the artist had been transferred onto the canvas. But it wasn't a *picture-perfect* butterfly. It was the *essence* of a butterfly, and perhaps even the essence of Sadie.

Then, something caused Sadie to look up. I observed her head scan the room and stop in the direction of Lucy's drawing. The doubt was palpable. Her head bent down toward her drawing, lifted to look at Lucy's, looked down again at her drawing, and back to Lucy's. She tried to wipe her hands off on her pants, and the colors just smeared more. She changed tactics, looking for different colors—colors that resembled

Lucy's. And I watched Sadie destroy her beautiful butterfly and produce a terrible copy of Lucy's. Worse yet, the kids next to Sadie saw her change in strategy and soon the entire table had followed suit, painting lousy renditions of Lucy's "picture-perfect" butterfly.

There are many c-words. I won't list them here but I'm sure you can fill in the blanks and get some negative attention if you say them out loud. But there is one c-word that outweighs them all in consequence. It is the drink of death for any artist—the word is "*compare.*"

Comparison is like kryptonite for your Superman or Superwoman creative soul. It crumbles, shrivels, and destroys your inspiration.

"Whatever you do, don't do the c-word. It will kill ya!"

I teach all my students that comparing is dangerous. Rarely does anything good come from it. Even I, who am experienced in avoiding the c-word, have to pull myself off Pinterest and other social media platforms because, as I sift through the myriads of paintings, my brain says, *Oh my goodness, these are amazing. I should do that. Oh, look at that! Why haven't I done that?* The noise that comes from comparing can be lethal to my artistic spirit. The moment I look over to Lucy's paper and allow the doubt to creep in, my artistic flow is in danger of being squelched.

Now, let me clarify. There *is* a time when it is okay to copy and even compare. But it should be done intentionally and sparingly. It takes some soul-searching to determine when you're ready for the c-word. Here are some questions to ask yourself:

1. Am I trying to learn a new skill or technique? *Healthy.*
2. Am I judging myself as an artist? *Unhealthy.*
3. Am I feeling inadequate, silly, childish, or behind? *Unhealthy.*
4. Am I recognizing differences and enjoying diversity? *Healthy.*
5. Am I excited by someone else's process? *Healthy.*
6. Am I enjoying someone else's progress? *Healthy.*
7. Am I feeling anxious or stressed by someone else's work? *Unhealthy.*

The key is that if you can keep your art and your artistic journey separated from who you are, it frees you up to compare without hindering your growth. In fact, when you can do this, the c-word can become a good word.

For example, when you first start painting or drawing, copying another artist will help you acquire new techniques and ideas. All the greatest artists copied as part of their studies before developing their own style. It's meant to be a stage of development as an artist, the hope being that, as you gain mastery of those techniques, you'll become more independent and "find your voice" organically. So, when you start to paint, pick paintings or pictures that you love and learn to copy them. In the art world, when you make a copy, we call it "a study"—which is just what it says.

Over time, you start to mix things up a bit. Maybe you feel brave enough to add something new to a copied painting. Then, as you continue to change this or that, you merge paintings and styles over time. The idea of copying is to learn techniques but soon your own style will emerge.

I love hyperrealism but I am far from being a hyperrealist painter. I don't have the focus or the time to sit for an hour and work on painting each eyelash on an eye. I can appreciate it, but it doesn't mean that I need to paint like that. It certainly doesn't mean that

I'm not a good painter or I'm not valid as an artist. If I compared my abstract dancers to a hyperrealist artist, however, I might start picking my own paintings apart, which would eventually lead to my judging myself as an artist.

Figuring out who you are, embracing it, and improving to become the best *you* that you can be while admiring others who are different is totally healthy. Admiring and feeling bad that you aren't like another person is not healthy.

My parents instilled in me a good sense of independence as well as self-confidence. It may have been their greatest gift to me. There wasn't much that I couldn't do if I wanted to. I never realized how their influence and confidence in me helped to build me into the person I am today. I believed that everyone felt the way I did but I'm finding that isn't true. I wish I could take the confidence my parents gave me and use it as an injection, pumping up everyone around me so they can feel the same way. Although I can't do that literally, I do my best to share that in my teaching.

My goal is to help each person find their own voice—their own style—and develop into the best they can possibly be. If you come into my studio for any Art-Women-Wine session, you will see that everyone is doing their own thing. We have a tradition that when you finish a painting, you must stand in front of the barn doors so I can take your picture and ring the cowbell. At that moment, everyone in class begins to cheer and give accolades for your accomplishment. Even the shyest of people must ring the bell and listen to the rest of the group bombard them with compliments. Soon, people skip to the bell with delight and can't wait to ring it. Regardless of how far along they are in their journey as an artist, they accomplished a piece and deserve some praise and support. It's a beautiful thing to see how each person does something different and yet they all support and encourage one another. Keeping that c-word in its proper place—to celebrate differences and uniqueness—is essential.

I always point out my students' earlier work and remind them of their growth as artists. I also let them know that our journeys as artists are different. For some, they speed right through and grow fast, while others are slow and steady. There is no right way to get there—in the quest to be an artist. The tortoise and the hare both win.

Comparison is like kryptonite for your Superman or Superwoman creative soul. It crumbles, shrivels, and destroys your inspiration.

So, what about real life? Have I played the comparison game? Unfortunately, yes. After my breakup with Sam, I started noticing all the wonderful relationships around me. You know, it's like when you buy a new red car, and you start to notice all the red cars on the road? Well, this can happen in the opposite way as well. I noticed all the couples who had long and wonderful marriages. I reminisced about my grandparents' fiftieth wedding anniversary and how they celebrated by taking the whole family to Chile. We saw where my dad grew up and where they served as missionaries many years prior. It was a fabulous time, a celebration of their lasting commitment to each other. Oh! How jealous I felt of their lifelong companionship.

My sister had also won the lottery with her husband, Paul. He is kind, handsome, a wonderful Christian, and so much fun! He showed up at our house on a road trip with his buddy, Donald Miller, back in 1993, when they were in their early 20s. Donald even wrote a book about it, *Through Painted Deserts,* which is a wonderful story of two young men on a quest across the country. Donald and Danielle had been pen pals for years and he decided to stop by to see her and introduce her to Paul. Paul fell fast and hard for my sister. To my credit, I prompted her to check out the "hot, surfer-looking dude" who was hanging out and tinkering on his Volkswagen bus in our driveway. A little competition (even though I probably didn't have a chance) from her little sis' prompted her to perk up and pay attention.

It's a good thing she did. Now, they were looking forward to their twentieth wedding anniversary in a few years, raising four beautiful girls, and enjoing a lifetime of love together. My parents also rounded their fortieth anniversary milestone together and it was yet another reminder of what I didn't have. Plan A had totally failed, and these reminders just kept showing up.

Then, there was one of my best friends, Catherine, who had a similar fate with her marriage early on in life, just like me, but then she found Henry. Her Prince Charming showed up and, unlike most of my love-interests, he lived in the same country. In fact, he lived just down the street. So even for Catherine, Plan B came fast, and it all worked out so beautifully, like a fairytale. To this day, they are still enjoying a wonderful companionship and marriage together.

I would be lying if I told you that I haven't been angry, jealous, envious, sad and even felt a sense of loss in this area of my life. There have been many cries out to God, even some clenched fists and cussing going on (I do repent) as to why my Plan A (getting married and staying married for a lifetime) didn't work out? It seemed like a cruel joke that God would allow me to experience a beautiful love with Sam (Plan B), only to have that not pan out as well.

Then, I remembered what I wrote in Weston's baby book, "I want to show you the world." During my seventeen years of marriage, I had not traveled abroad. Since the divorce, I created my trips to Italy. And now in a matter of just a few years I had been to *il bel paese* several times, Spain, and even Morocco. I brought my kids to Italy, indeed showing them the world, for an entire summer. My art business was growing. I created a thriving community for my Art-Women-Wine ladies as well as for my Art-Van-Go kids. I had created some of my most powerful paintings to date during this time. I used all that sadness and channeled that grief into my artwork and life, and it's been wonderful.

I'm not saying that I would wish bad things like infidelity or a divorce on anyone. What I am saying is, if you stop comparing and focus on your own path, you can create something new, amazing and different. God used my circumstances to break me open and showed me his plan which is better than anything I could ever imagine. I may never get to celebrate my fiftieth golden wedding anniversary, but I have won gold as a mom, an artist, and an inspiration to so many through my teaching and travels. The truth is, when I look back, I wouldn't change a thing. I am grateful for this life, where my Plan A and Plan B have failed, but where God's plan never fails. I can't wait for the rest of MY STORY and what's next for me.

Chapter 11:

Make a Sloppy Copy

During indoor restrictions from the COVID-19 pandemic, I had to change tactics in how I instructed my Art-Women-Wine students. The difference wasn't just in the platform. Usually, students do their own thing and I act as more of a guide than an actual teacher. Teaching on zoom video conferencing, however, made continuing this format difficult. Instead, I decided to teach different techniques with a step-by-step approach. I argued that this would push them to learn something new and it was easier to orchestrate over zoom than trying to replicate the individualized instruction I was used to doing for in-person classes.

Molly is tall and athletic with crystal blue eyes and a smile that brightens a room. She is a dedicated swimmer and I know she is disciplined and determined to do anything she puts her mind to. She is already becoming a proficient painter in a very short time. Although the social isolation due to COVID-19 mandates was hard on her, Molly still showed up to zoom classes with a cheerful willingness to learn.

I taught several easier techniques in the beginning and then dove into more challenging concepts. I could see Molly's frustration grow. I realized that, with each lesson, she was aiming for a masterpiece. She was vexed because her skills weren't immediately translating into a strong, finished product. I could also see that she wasn't alone. I decided to intervene.

"Hey everyone," I said. "I'd like for each of you to remove all expectations of this first draft. You need to focus on just learning these techniques. Stop worrying about the outcome. You can master these concepts later with time."

The atmosphere shifted. I could even see a few students exhale in relief in their little zoom squares. I added, "Your goal should be to make a *sloppy copy* of what I'm doing so you become acquainted with what we're trying to learn." I learned the term "sloppy copy" from my my Art Van-Go students. We were doing something new, and I was trying to explain to them that this was just a rough draft.

One of the kids exclaimed, "Okay, Ms. Elida, great! This is just our sloppy copy." The name stuck.

The lesson that day with my Art-Women-Wine gals was more relaxed. The pressure was off, and they laughed and joked more. Interestingly, the women were able to go back and complete some fabulous paintings. For some, it may be their strongest group of paintings yet, and without any of my help.

Teaching different types of personalities is very challenging. I think it is like how people cook. For me, I may glance at a recipe, but I really view it as a suggestion. I never measure, just estimate. My sister, on the other hand, will measure by scraping off the teaspoon with a butter knife. This tends to work very well for baking and, admittedly, with most things. But the difference is that my dinners are always new—even if they are the same recipe—because I make the dish a little different each time. For those who crave variety, you can probably relate. Others have peace in knowing that they'll come up with the outcome they want by following the instructions closely.

The same goes for painting. You have some who want to follow a recipe. They try to carefully copy every stroke, get the same brushes and paint, and squirt exactly the right amount of paint out on the palette. Others just want a basic guideline. With acrylic painting, it's advantageous to be the second type. You must let go of a fixed outcome in your mind and be flexible. Because there are so many factors in painting, even if you follow the recipe, it might not be the same.

A sloppy copy is a brilliant way to think about anything you are learning that is new. We all need several rough drafts to get that finished piece. How many paintings have I created that really aren't masterpieces and how many paintings have I painted over? Too many to count. But it's important to note that each sloppy copy was essential in helping me paint a masterpiece. And the sloppy copies are no less important than the masterpiece because they are what propelled my growth. Without them, I could not have expanded and explored. I would have restricted myself to a formula.

I've discovered that kids are so much more open to the idea of sloppy copies. They are accustomed to trying and failing and not achieving perfection soon after they begin. Just watch a toddler, for instance. He attempts to climb the stairs to the slide and it's a disaster. You must help him, keep your hand on him, and teach him until he gets it and then he'll do it over again. You see him smile and say, "Again, again, again!"

As we get older, we should keep that same enthusiasm as we learn something new. You don't see that toddler putting himself down about how slow or cumbersome he is as he tries to climb. He is too intent on learning. That excitement, and the possibility of success, propels him to keep at it.

When I first started to salsa dance, I knew nothing. I went with a group of my *gringa* girlfriends—who knew less about dancing than I did—to a dive joint called the Cha Cha Club. We walked through a sports bar with big TVs, a stage for rock bands, pitchers of beer sloshing on tables, and loud-mouthed men sitting and staring at screens. This wasn't my vibe. But then there was a stairwell that led to the basement. The venue was dark and gritty with low ceilings, a small stage, and dimly lit bathrooms but it was packed with salsa dancers and the music was blasting—it was magical.

I had no formal dance training other than a few tap lessons my mom put me into because I was always a little too beefy for ballet. My girlfriends and I tried our best to dance hip-hop to the music. It was a flop. For those of you who don't know anything about salsa, it's a partner dance with the man leading and the woman following. So, dancing individually with your girlfriends in a circle kind of sets you apart in an awkward way. Moreover, a salsa rhythm basically consists of taking three steps for every four beats of music. The odd number of steps creates a syncopation. All that to say, hip-hop dancing wasn't working at all. But we forged ahead, grasping at the beat like a fish out of water gasping for air.

Soon, a Mexican man decided to rescue me and whisked me onto the dance floor. He introduced himself as Solo Vino, which means *only wine.* I took Solo Vino's hand, and he transformed me into a salsa queen. Spinning, twirling, and flipping me over his back in one swoosh, my feet barely even touched the ground. My hair was flying, and I was sweating. Somehow, my feet were moving without me knowing any of the moves. Looking back, I'm sure I looked a lot like that toddler on the slide but like that toddler with a big smile, I exclaimed, "Again, again, again!" and I never stopped. Although my knees might keep me from performing professionally, my sloppy copy of salsa dancing improved to become something beautiful and satisfying and so will yours. Whenever you start something new, remember to keep your confidence and determination like that of a baby. Maybe even write yourself a note that says "again, again, again," and soon you'll be smiling!

I've discovered that kids are more open to the idea of sloppy copies. They are accustomed to trying and failing and not achieving perfection soon after they begin.

After my breakup with Sam, I started going to therapy. My therapist helped me to get some perspective on my past dating experiences. Why did I keep choosing guys that were … geographically distant, emotionally unavailable, or downright dangerous? Why did I walk into a crowded room and find myself immediately and irresistibly drawn to someone who was just plain wrong for me?

She suggested that I imagine this scene: I walk into an exciting salsa dance club. I scan the room and I catch someone's eyes as he is dancing. Our eyes lock. My feet move toward him without my even telling them to, his magnetism is so powerful. I look back at my friends, hoping one of them will grab my hand, pull me back because I know this isn't going to go well. But no one rescues me, and I keep walking toward him. When I get close to him, I smile and ...

I look past him to another guy who is sitting at one of the tables, drinking a beer with his friends.

"That's your guy, Elida," my therapist says. "You need to realize that the man in the center of the dance floor isn't going to work out. He's not real. He's not right. It's the guy on the sidelines who is relationship material."

Ugh! Just thinking through the scene caused me to go through a roller coaster of emotions: excitement, attraction, power, and ... what was it that I felt at the end when I saw the guy on the sidelines? Fear and disappointment. I realized that perhaps I was afraid of starting something real with someone. I wanted excitement. I wanted danger. I wanted novelty. And perhaps, deep down, I didn't want things to last.

My therapist was so right. I confessed to her that, on my calendar, I had a trip planned to see Mr. Mountain Dew in Arizona. Like the famous soda-pop commercials, he was one of those hot guys who jumped off docks into lakes, water skied, and lived the outdoorsy fun life. He had long wavy hair to his shoulders, played guitar in a band on the weekend, taught history during the week, and lived on a boat! He had played professional baseball and football in Europe and had just returned from Germany. So here he was asking me to come down for a visit to see him.

In desperation, I asked my therapist, "What the heck am I supposed to do?"

She shut me down. "Look, you can keep doing what you've been doing. And you'll keep getting what you're getting. Or you can try my idea. Try dating a guy who is different from your usual attractions. Maybe, just maybe, you'll like it and it'll work."

Meanwhile, at salsa dancing, I was doing my thang. Sweaty and breathless, I escaped the dance floor for a second to catch my breath and grab a drink of water at the water station. A tall, dark, and handsome man with a big smile leaned in and said, "*Quieres bailar*?" As I was gulping down my water, I could see my therapist shaking her head no! He was everything I should avoid. But, of course, I nodded my head. Then, he leaned back away from the bar and held his hand toward another man— taller, darker and with an even bigger smile. He grabbed this guy's arm and pushed him towards me while he was still sipping his beer, saying, "Dance with my friend!"

My therapist would be pleased. He literally was the guy in the corner— not dancing, kind of shy, and just drinking a beer. He was quiet and unassuming, with dark curly hair that stood up all over the place, in a good way, and eye lashes that extended clear up to his eyebrows. He had a kind face and an athletic build. Woah, was he ever hot, and how had I never seen him before? My therapist's voice came into my head. *It's because you're always looking in the middle of the dance floor and not paying attention to the sidelines.*

"Hola, me llamo Elida," I said.

He smiled and kissed my cheek in greeting, "*Hola, me llamo Alex. Mi madre tiene el mismo nombre.*" (My mom has the same name).

I chuckled. *Nice pickup line,* I thought. I had never met anyone with my name. "No, no, my name is spelled, E-L-I-D-A." He smiled again and pulled out his phone to show me. There it was: "Elida. Mi Madre."

Was it fate? Or a coincidence? At minimum, it was worth a dance. Was I brave enough to make a sloppy copy of dating the guy in the corner like my therapist suggested? I wasn't sure yet. We danced throughout the night, and I learned he was from the Dominican Republic and had played professional baseball. We chatted about my kids playing baseball and I found out he was new to the area. At the end of the evening, I slipped him my business card before grabbing my jacket. I stood on my toes, kissed his cheek and said, "I don't date salsa guys. It's a rule, but we can be friends."

He smiled and replied, "Well, I never asked you out on a date, but I'm happy you gave me your number. I'd like to be friends." I don't get embarrassed often, but sometimes I get flustered. I was still pretty set on my trip to see Mr. Mountain Dew and I don't like breaking my rules, but this encounter had me thinking deep down, *I hope he calls.*

Chapter 12:

When in Doubt, Add Another Layer

Ally moved to Camas from California. She has a very artistic daughter, Gabrielle, whom she immediately signed up for art classes. Then, she discovered Art-Women-Wine classes and decided to give art a try for herself. Eventually, she became more involved with painting than Gabrielle did, as swimming and school competed for her daughter's time. Ally has red hair and is bright, bubbly, and straightforward. There's no guesswork as to whether she likes something or not —I really like that about her.

Ally began working on a new painting. The goal was to have a textured background with a woman sitting with her back toward the viewer, looking off to the side, in the forefront. She struggled with it for a long time. The back was wrong. Then the head was off, the arm looked fat, and the hips were askew. Week in and week out she changed the positioning, shading, and color, and still the piece didn't move forward. After many classes and failed attempts, I asked her, "Do you like this painting?"

Ally glared, unimpressed with my question, and said, "Do I look like I'm having fun? I hate it!"

I walked over to her seat, handed her a palette knife, and said, "Then paint over it." A grin spread over her face, slightly evil, and Ally began to mix all kinds of brilliant colors. With big, thick, bold strokes, she covered the entire canvas. The colors were so "Ally," and the thick texture was exactly what she wanted. The painting (although no longer a woman, dreamily looking to the side) was now something that made her smile, and something that she loved, not hated. There is such freedom in knowing you can add another layer to parts of your painting or cover everything up with a layer over the top.

With watercolors, you must know the finished product before starting your piece. As a medium, they are unforgiving. You must establish where your lights will be from the beginning and you'd better not touch them because, once you lose your whites, you'll never get them back. With acrylics, there is ample mercy and grace to mess up or change course. In fact, half the time I don't know where I'm going with a piece until I start painting. I decide what I'm painting as I see something form in the process.

I remember a visit to my Grandma Dottie. She had finished a huge painting of a horse. The next visit, the same-sized canvas was sitting in the same place, but it was a painting of Portofino.

I asked, "Where did you move your horse painting?"

She answered, "He's in there! Right under Portofino. I painted over him. I got tired of the way he was looking at me!" That was it. It didn't matter if people liked the painting. It didn't matter if it was good, or she could have sold it. She didn't like it, so she fearlessly painted over the top of it.

I use that method quite often. When I'm painting my dancers, I always start painting legs in different positions. Soon, she will start to look like "Octomom" with multiple legs going all over the place. I don't worry about it because I know that's how I paint and that's how acrylics work. You just keep painting and eventually, between the mistakes and multiple legs, you find something that's good. The point is to keep going.

It's not that the layers underneath don't mean anything or weren't necessary. Every stroke and every mistake were needed to help you find what the painting was intended to be.

Sometimes I daydream that I'm standing on a little piece of floating rock or ice. It's only slightly wider than my feet and it's flat, like a steppingstone. I'm way above the clouds and there's nothing around me. I can't see anything for miles. An inner voice tells me to just step off and a new step will appear. But it's so scary. It's a long fall if nothing is there. I wait for a long time and, finally, I step off the stone. As soon as I step off, a new step shoots up and meets my foot right at the exact second, I would fall. Then, I take the next step and *swoosh!* A new step appears. Soon, I'm moving at lightning speed above the heavens.

I've gotten stuck standing there while facing my canvas, too afraid to start. When this happens, I do the artist's version of stepping off into the void. I may swipe a big swish of color across the canvas or scribble something in chalk. The scariest part is that first step, so I just get it over with. When I reach another plateau, *swish!* I swab on another splash of color. This art of releasing control and boldly, even cavalierly, just slapping color on is often the action we should take. It breaks the tension. It cuts the resistance. It slashes the fear. Because movement, no matter how small, means you are fighting. It shows you're alive and it signals to everyone, including yourself, that you are not defeated.

Sometimes, I've had to transfer what I've learned in art to other creative endeavors. For instance, it's always been a dream of mine to write a book, but I would always think, *I'm not a writer; I'm an artist!* My sister encouraged me to just start writing but I didn't have a plan or any idea how to get started.

As I began to talk to her about all these art lessons and how each pertains to life, she said, "Now there's your book!" It was the step rising to meet my foot. I wouldn't have even known how to begin but I just started writing what I knew, adding another layer, and then another. Soon I could see how these random stories all fit together and now, here you are reading it!

Ally glared, unimpressed with my question, and said, "Do I look like I'm having fun? I hate it! I walked over to her seat, handed her a palette knife, and said, "Then paint over it."

As I jumped on the plane to see Mr. Mountain Dew, I knew I was walking straight toward the guy in the middle of the dance floor. I felt conflicted. All the excitement was there as well as the guilt and the sense of doom that I had seen and done this all before— only the scenery had changed. We sailed through the red rocks at Lake Powell where we got caught in a rainstorm and had to snuggle down below in the boat. I watched him play in the band every night at this honky-tonk bar where I ate steak and danced to country music. We had long talks late into the night and spent a lot of time laying on the boat and looking at the stars. It was magical.

Then, it was time for me to go. We drove through Zion National Park where the curved rocks and desert landscape was so vast and gorgeous, it took my breath away. He got me to the airport late, so it was a quick kiss and goodbye. I raced in only to realize I had missed my flight.

I called him back immediately because all I could think of was that we would get a little more time together.

He answered, "Hey, what's going on, everything ok?"

Me: "Yes, and no. The bad news is I missed my flight, but the good news is that we get a few more hours together?"

There was silence on the other end. Then, he reluctantly replied, "Oh, dang! I was planning on trying to get back to play in the band tonight. Let me see what I can do. I'll call ya back."

He was able to rearrange his schedule for the night, but something felt off. Here we had this romantic weekend together and I wanted him to be excited to see me. I wanted him to make a U-turn and come racing back, but instead it felt like an obligation and more of an annoyance to him. There was also the fact that he didn't even acknowledge that the reason I missed my flight was because he dropped me off late. The evening continued. We went out to eat, enjoyed our time together, but I could tell he was antsy and wanting to get back. I left feeling a little disappointed.

After I got home, we stayed in touch, but

he wasn't calling me as much as I hoped. I certainly wasn't feeling pursued. I liked him a lot and I thought he felt the same, but I guess I was mistaken.

Meanwhile, I was busy remodeling my 1910 craftsman house with my dad. We had just one month to get all the finish work done and it was crunch time. The tall, dark, and handsome man from salsa had stayed in touch and volunteered to help. He would show up after his regular job as a handyman every day and work alongside my dad late into the evenings. I could hear them chattering away in Spanish and laughing as they worked into the night. When my dad tried to pay him, he refused and said he was happy to help me out. The only payment he wanted was getting a little more time to see me. Each night when he left, he'd give me a goodbye kiss on the cheek.

I was still talking with Mr. Mountain Dew, wishing that a relationship with him looked more promising. A few weeks later I went to lunch at Costco with a bunch of ladies from my Art-Women-Wine class. By this time, we had all become friends and sometimes after class we'd run and go grocery shopping or out to eat together. As I was biting into my chicken bake, I complained, "I don't know what to do. I've got this guy in Arizona who I really like, but even after our amazing time together, he isn't calling me much."

Debra looked over at me as she blotted her chin from the cheese of her pepperoni pizza. "And you've got Sweet Chocolate Dominican Goodness who has been helping your dad and you for the past few months and showing up at your boys' baseball games to support you."

I slurped down my cappuccino, "Yeah, but we met at salsa, and you know my rule about not dating salsa guys."

Kristen licked the mustard off her finger from her hotdog and said, "Well, sometimes you have to break your own rules, Elida. Pay attention to who showed up to the party! You've got this guy in Arizona who's not really pursuing you and you're making all the effort. Then you've got this guy here who you've given nothing to, and he just keeps showing up."

All right, ladies, I thought. *And copy, therapist.* It was time to paint over all these past efforts at making the guy in the center of the dance floor the center of my attention. I'm done! That day at the Costco food court I decided to give Sweet Chocolate and my therapist's suggestion a chance. My dating life was getting a fresh coat of paint. Who knew, maybe this could turn into a masterpiece?

Chapter 13:

Be Fearless, Sometimes

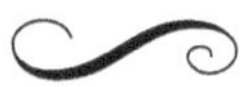

"How can I make my building look three-dimensional and have texture like the old-world buildings of Europe?" asked Sarah.

I thought for a minute and then exclaimed, "Why don't we put real stucco on that building?" Sarah looked reluctant as I pulled out the bucket of stucco patch from under the red rolling table. This wasn't a product from the art supply store and there was nothing on the label that indicated that it could be used for a painting, but as I pried off the lid with a screwdriver, she shrugged her shoulders and nodded her assent. With a palette knife, I showed her how she could add depth and authenticity to her structure.

I knew that this technique would work because I had already tested it. After a few failed attempts at using other construction materials, I found the solution. I had also discovered that there was only one hardware store in town that carried stucco patch, it took a long time to dry, but it looked fabulous when it was done. I spent the rest of the class sharing my "Technique Tuesday" tip with the group. Sarah ended up stuccoing her building and the result was stunning.

Art and invention often go together. Often, it's hard to know where one begins and the other ends. Was Claude Monet, when he decided to leave off reproducing scenes and attempted to capture the impression of a moment, an inventor or an artist? Or when Picasso decided to leap off the cliff of all his past training to "paint like a child." Artist or inventor? Even Einstein attributes the discovery of that well-known formula to intuition and inspiration rather than logic or mathematics.

Being an artist means trying new things. This is one of our superpowers; it can also be our kryptonite. There's a fine line between being brave and being reckless. I learned this painful lesson when I decided to paint a giant mural on my round cement patio next to my art studio. Because I wanted a more permanent painting on my patio, I decided to paint my own version of Botticelli's *Venus* using acrylics so they would last. She would be spectacular, a figure that was ten feet tall. Everyone who walked by on the sidewalk above could peek through my Italian cypresses and see her in all her glory! She would be the envy of all my neighbors.

I was so excited to start the project that I jumped right in without planning it out. Fall was coming fast and, where I live, that meant rain was coming. I reasoned that the canvas of cement wouldn't be any different than a canvas of cloth. I would paint with acrylic paints and then seal it when I finished, right? I would finish the face first and let it dry. Then, I would work on the hair and body later. I chose the next sunny day to get started and completed my beautiful Venus's face. As I washed out my paint brushes, I felt confident that I would be able to complete her within the week.

But the next day, it rained. Heavily. To my dismay, my painting began to wash away. My poor, beautiful Venus looked like she'd had a stroke! Her mouth was sliding down on the side of her cheek and pockmarks from the rain took paint off all over her face. When I saw her from the sidewalk, I cried. All that work, time, and effort was gone! I clearly had not done my research, and now I was forced to go back to the beginning. I researched cement, paints, and sealers and figured out how to save what I had already created. First, I built a tent around my Venus. Then, I had ditches and canals built in the yard around her to divert the water. I bought heaters, special sealers, and more paints. It was a mess. At some point in the process, when my reference papers were soaking wet, my ditches were full of water, and I was freezing cold and had mud splattered all over me, I looked at my painting and yelled, "You bitch, Venus!" It made me feel better calling her names even if it wasn't her fault. She and I had wrestled for weeks.

Eventually, she surrendered to becoming beautiful. I won. She is such a surprise for those passing by. When I'm standing in front of my kitchen window, I enjoy watching people's faces as they discover this miraculous piece of art in an unexpected place. Joy springs up in my heart when I see them smile and point at my beautiful Venus.

I have another circle cement patio on which I would love to paint one more muse. Maybe I'll paint Frida Kahlo or Georgia O'Keefe, two of my favorite modern artists. But this time, I will do things differently. I will start earlier in the summer, and I will prepare the cement before I dive into the painting. I will seal it and it will last--probably better than my first one and certainly with a lot less heartache. This is the artist/inventor process.

If you've ever been to Florence, Italy, you probably have seen the chalk artists who can recreate beautiful masterpieces on the cobblestone streets. They produce the paintings of Botticelli's stunning *Venus* in a much bigger rendition, or they'll bring to life Leonardo's *Mona Lisa*, and they do it in just one day! It's a wonderful experience to walk by in the morning and return that night to see them finishing their masterpieces. Chalk is a temporary medium, and I am so sad to see that the next morning the street sweepers washed them away. I never actually quite understood this—to create something so beautiful that won't last. However, as I'm getting older, I'm realizing that the process of creating is one of the most beautiful gifts that we can give to ourselves and the world. It's the journey that brings us the most joy and if you are lucky enough to create a strong painting that lasts—well, that's a bonus!

In *The Agony and the Ecstasy,* author Irving Stone describes the rivalry between Michelangelo and Leonardo da Vinci. Da Vinci had been commissioned by the *signoria* or government to paint a giant panel in the main city hall. When Michelangelo heard about this, he was furious. He thought himself to be the best artist in the world. Why had he been passed over? He stormed into the city hall and demanded that they hire him for the second panel. He took the commission at a fraction of the amount, but he didn't care because it was more important for the world to recognize that he was the superior artist. Da Vinci did his panel first but being an inventor, he tried to apply an ancient encaustic style of painting on a massive scale. While applying heat to the top half of the mural, the lower half melted away. Soon after, Michelangelo was called away to work on the Pope's tomb and both projects were abandoned.

Recently, I was commissioned to paint two beautiful paintings and signs on the wood floor of a clothing boutique store, Lily Atelier. Again, I was so eager to get painting that I forgot my lesson about Venus a few years before. I began painting directly on the wood floor. What could go wrong with painting on wood? The acrylics will stick, right? I soon discovered that the oil sealer on the floor repelled all the acrylic paint, and it *wasn't* sticking. I ran down to the local hardware store for sandpaper and had to start over. Luckily, I learned this early on before getting too far into the project and saved myself a lot of heartache. The painting would have just rubbed off and, like Da Vinci, I would have had a disappearing painting.

After resolving the issue of the sealant repelling my paint, I whipped right through the painting of my first woman and holding the sign. However, when I put the polyurethane sealer on it, it smeared the writing on the sign instead of sealing it. I learned that using Aquavar first and then adding the sealer would do the trick. Next, onto the second woman. Although I had to sand more because the wood was newer, she turned out very pretty with her hat and gloves on.

That is, until I got to her face. I finished painting for the day, but I knew she wasn't right. So, the next day, I headed back to the painting and sanded the entire face off. That's right, a full-face remodel! I asked the owner, "Please, don't look during this process because it's ugly and scary while in the process but so necessary to get the results we are after." In the end, I made the most beautiful face, and the head was finally right even though it took me a total facial reconstruction. I signed it and sealed it and now the women of Lily Atelier are there for everyone to see and admire!

Being an artist means trying new things. This is one of our superpowers; it can also be our kryptonite. There's a fine line between being brave and being reckless."

In art and life, it's important to make a run at the goal. To strike. To aim at creating something big and bold. But it's also important to do a little planning. To experiment small before going big. To try a new technique when the stakes aren't huge.

I tried to be both brave and smart when beginning a relationship with Alex. There was so much to overcome. We came from different cultures and family backgrounds. Our base languages were different, and we had a lot of laughable moments when things got lost in translation. Our belief systems were different too.

I asked him a lot of questions and listened intently to the answers, but maybe I should have listened to the questions he asked of me.

"Can you have more kids?" I took it as a direct question as to whether my ovaries were still working, which at the time they were working just fine.

"Yes," I said, not really thinking about the implications of the question.

There were other things too that should have been red flags. There was that strange text message, an unusual charge on his phone, and other things that seemed suspicious. But wasn't this trust issue my problem, the old baggage from the past?

But when we danced *bachata* together, it was as if the angels were singing! Our bodies moved in perfect harmony; everything synchronized from our heads to our toes. Our hips aligned and he rested his wrist on the top of my hip directing me. Our faces touched, cheek to cheek, and if you could hear our heartbeats, I am certain that even they fell into rhythm. There was magic between us. That connection kept us glued together.

Our lives became more intertwined. I launched a fundraiser to help him get his citizenship. Soon, we celebrated him as a citizen of the United States of

America. He started traveling with me and became a helpful, integral part of my tours. Then, his apartment lease was up, and it didn't really make sense to renew it. All that money wasted. Our lives were enmeshed and the idea of not doing life together seemed awful. I loved him deeply.

Suddenly, it dawned on me that I had done it again. I had jumped into the relationship with both feet, and I was too invested to be truly logical and reasonable about whether it was a good idea to move forward. I argued to myself that my counselor suggested I try looking at someone different for a change and Alex was not like the guys I usually dated. He was literally the guy I overlooked on the dance floor. I was just following my therapist's advice, right?

Just like my Venus, I had committed to a huge project without really doing my research. I was trying to paint acrylics on a brand-new surface. Should I sand it off and start over or keep plugging away? Was it premature? Was this experiment going to pan out or was it going to become a face sliding off the canvas?

Chapter 14:

It's the Dark Darks That Make the Brights Bright

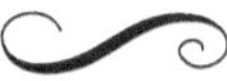

"Why won't my painting pop?" Kelly complained. "I want my flower to be brighter. I keep adding lighter colors, but the painting just keeps getting worse!"

I came over to look at the canvas. Large blocks of white lay flat on the canvas. They were supposed to be petals, but they didn't even look like a flower. She had tried to make her flower look more three-dimensional by adding white paint over the top to no avail—the blocks of paint remained lifeless.

"Do you trust me?" I asked. Kelly nodded, a little unsure, but she handed me the brush. I took her palette and mixed up a rich black and a dark gray. As I began heavily painting over her white flower with bold strokes, I heard a sharp intake of breath. A few sideways glances revealed that her wine was disappearing rather quickly. When I finished and put down the paintbrush, I detected a drip of sweat forming on her forehead.

She set her wine glass down and said sarcastically, "Well, thank you, Elida. Now I have a *death* flower!" We laughed and I tried to comfort her with a hug and a promise that it would turn out okay. I told her to take a break while the paint dried and then we would start anew.

When she returned, we built the color of the flower up again with brighter colors. This time, the wrinkles in the petals and edges appeared crisp against the background. When we were finished, that pop of color she desired erupted on the canvas. She stepped back, and I heard another intake of breath—this time I knew that sound expressed a completely different emotion. Kelly was ecstatic with the outcome. Her flower bloomed with brilliance. It was a turning point for her as an artist, the moment she fell in love with painting. And she continues to paint to this day.

As she hugged me and gave a sincere thank you instead of a sarcastic one, I said, "Remember this lesson, Kelly. It's the dark darks that make the brights bright!"

"Well, thank you, Elida," she said sarcastically. "Now I have a *death* flower!"

In acrylics, you should almost always paint the dark colors first. Then, add lighter colors, leaving the brightest, whitest colors for the end. If the base is dark, then the dark colors of the crevices, cracks, crinkles, and wrinkles that you want to add to the painting are already there, which makes it easier to highlight edges and reflections. Otherwise, you end up trying to push darkness into the tiny places rather than having them emerge naturally. It gives the painting depth.

To make a really dramatic statement, put the deepest, darkest color next to the brightest and lightest color. New painters often mistakenly think that if they want a light painting, they must use only light colors. They haven't learned or have forgotten that the contrast makes the bright colors shine.

Have you ever been in a dark space with no light? Then, when a sliver of light peeks through, it is incredibly bright. Blinding, almost. But that same sliver of light might not be noticed at all in an already lit room.

This applies to our lives as well. When I went through a separation with my ex-husband for the second time, I cried until there were no more tears left to cry. I wondered whether my body would just give up. To me, divorce felt like someone took a giant, dull spoon, cut into my stomach just below my rib cage and scooped out all my insides, strewing the sadness and emptiness, the unfulfilled hopes, and broken dreams over the floor for me to stare at. It was the most grueling thing I've experienced. There were days when I didn't want to get up. Many times, I woke up wishing that the pain was just a dream. I can't speak to everyone's difficult times. I know others have endured so much more than me. I wish I could take it all away, but I can't.

The beautiful thing about painting with acrylics is that even the darkest darks can be painted over, and all the dark layers underneath add texture, richness, and depth to the painting. Nothing in your life has been in vain; it can all be transformed into something beautiful. We often want to forget or avoid the dark times or hide them under a mask of light colors. The problem is that when we do that, we also hide our true, authentic selves. We're not allowing people to see who we are. There is no darkness so dark that God's love can't shine upon it. We get to decide whether we are willing to let the master's hand work in our lives.

Sometimes we feel that our lives are simply missing depth—missing that pop of color—and we keep doing things repeatedly with the same result. Then, the master painter walks by and asks, "Do you trust me?" We choose whether to hand the paintbrush to him and see what he will do. I guarantee it's going to be different from what we expected. At the same time, it will be exactly what we need.

All the dark layers underneath add texture, richness, and depth to the painting. Nothing in your life has been in vain; it can all be transformed into something beautiful.

Most of you who are reading this book are in a first-world culture, which means you're probably used to comfort. We Americans have what I call "sixty-eight-degree syndrome." Our houses are set at sixty-eight degrees or whatever temperature we deem comfortable. When we leave our temperature-controlled homes, we get into our temperature-controlled cars and head to our temperature-controlled offices. Our showers are hot. Our drinking water is cold. We have medications readily available for any discomfort, whether it's a mild headache or severe depression. If we are bored, we can use Wi-Fi and our phones to numb out. To sum up, we are accustomed to easy living, and if we stay too long in a completely comfortable world, we will miss out on the dark darks that are needed to give our lives depth and meaning. It also means we miss out on those bright brights, too.

I was reminded of this when I visited Alex's family in Palo Verde, a small, rural town in the northwest corner of the Dominican Republic near the Haitian border. As someone who has visited Europe numerous times, I always believed I was a good traveler, someone who could not only endure the disconcerting differences from American life with ease but also embrace them with gusto. I thought the late trains were a good time to chat it up with the locals, the cramped seats were charming, the tepid water was healthier, and the bathroom down the hall of my hotel was quaint.

On my trip to Palo Verde, however, I was faced with a new level of unsettling circumstances. On my first attempt at a shower, I yelled out, "Honey, there is no hot water!"

He laughed and said, "Mammie, there is no hot water in the whole town!" I stood there as the frigid water trickled out barely splashing my feet and wanted to cry. I finally gathered my courage and ducked under the drizzle for the world's most miserable shower ever. And every shower after that was again the world's most miserable shower ever.

When we finally arrived at a hotel in the bigger city of Puerto Plata, I looked forward to a real, bona fide shower. I was so excited because, after playing all day at the beach, I had sand in every crevice of my body. But Alex's four-year-old daughter needed to shower first because she had to eat dinner and get to bed soon. When I finally finished washing her up, I wrapped her in a towel and sent her out, eager for my turn to clean up. I stepped into the shower only to feel the terrible, familiar feeling of…yes, you guessed it, freezing cold water! While Alex dealt with Laney's fit as she resisted dinner and bedtime, I had my own temper tantrum for not getting a hot shower. I almost packed my bags and left the country.

A few days later, I discovered that, not only was there no hot water, but there also wasn't any water at all! The power was gone too. I panicked. Again, I shouted the obvious, my eyes wide in horror, "Alex, there's no water and no electricity!"

He just laughed again, shrugging his shoulders, as if this were no surprise. In fact, it was a common occurrence. "Yeah, none in the whole city today, but it will probably come back tomorrow."

Tomorrow? I thought. *Are you kidding me?* I decided to try again as if he didn't hear me correctly. "Alex, there's *no power!* Whom do we need to call to get this fixed? We might die! We can't live without water! How will we eat?"

Eventually, I learned that the region just rotates electricity from town to town, giving each city a turn for comfort for a while. Since most of the people don't really pay the electricity and water bills, the city shuts them down for a few days until enough people pay up to motivate them to turn the electricity back on. The locals were all used to this, but the poor princess American girl, who was certain she would die, was not at all used to this. I learned that the big barrels of water stored in the showers are for just such occasions. *I take a bucket of this and dump it in the toilet for an instant flush! Who knew?* I found myself hot, dirty, and uncomfortable.

Little did I know that this discomfort would be the background on my life's canvas to some amazing experiences. On it we painted the Christmas Eve celebration where we roasted two pigs and twenty-four chickens, rotating them on massive skewers over a giant fire pit while drinking rum throughout the night. There was the zip-lining trip in a monkey-inhabited jungle that my dad, boys, and I all screamed through. And the daily routine of driving through the rice fields, seeing the electrifying green color. Or there was that moment when, while walking along, Alex threw a rock at a tree that I thought was covered in white blooms. I watched the blooms leap into the air, becoming thousands of egrets. They spread across the blue sky in a vast pattern of pale plumes and necks and beaks and feet. Or there was the childish excitement of each member of Alex's family, regardless of age, receiving a Christmas gift from us (wrapped in tissue paper as that was all we could find). They don't usually give and receive gifts at Christmas time.

We facilitated and enjoyed watching Alex's nephew, Carlos, age six, play in the ocean for the first time (just a twenty-minute drive away). There was the time when I rode through the plantain fields on the back of a motorcycle, the sun shining on my face and the wind blowing through my hair like we were in a Corona beer commercial. Or when I painted a picture for Alex's mom in their backyard, surrounded by tropical trees and flowers. Or seeing my youngest son, Weston, glory in catching frogs, lizards, and geckos and watching baby chicks hatch.

These moments shine through my memory like beacons. I wonder whether I would remember them as vividly if my senses weren't awakened by the freezing cold showers! If we give ourselves fully over to experience the discomforts, we give space for the adventures to glow. It was after these times that we grew closer together. Tough experiences either bring you closer or tear you apart. It's always a good sign when you find yourself working as a team and overcoming challenges.

I challenge you to do a few things in your life that are uncomfortable. Maybe it's traveling or even something as simple as signing up for an art class (even if you don't feel like you're an artist). Maybe it's going to church for the first time or stating an opinion that might cause a little controversy. Remember, these uncomfortable experiences are the background. You are layering a dark layer so that when you put the brighter colors over the top, you will have a richer life that will really pop with color!

Chapter 15:

Know When to Stop

"Drop the paintbrush and back away from the painting!" I yelled across the studio.

Jen looked up at me from her amazing painting of abstract aspen trees in disbelief and asked, "Are you talking to me?"

"*Yes*, I am totally talking to you!"

Jen is constantly questioning herself. She thinks that there is no way she could just slap some paint on the canvas and have it all work out right away. She wants to feel the labor pains so she can be assured that her baby has really been born. The problem is that she is often done with the piece before she recognizes it and then she continues to paint. In the end, the piece looks overworked, and she regrets not stopping earlier.

Picasso said, "The artwork is always done before the artist believes it is." I've found that statement to be true on most occasions. Your gut tells you it's good, but your mind argues. You think, *If it is too easy, it must not be good.* There are sweet spots you hit in painting. Sometimes the sweet spots come early in the painting process, and you don't believe that the painting could be done because you haven't really sweated or worked on it enough.

Early in my painting career, my musician friend, Scott, and I practiced doing a live painting together. He played a song on his guitar, and I painted a giant painting in under five minutes. We were practicing for a live auction event where I would repeat the painting in front of a large audience and then we'd auction the piece off to help raise funds for our local schools.

When I was finished with our run-through, I threw the painting aside, planning to paint over it, until my colleague, Frank, saw it. "Elida, don't paint over that. It's good. It just needs some firmer lines in a few places, and it's done." I was shocked that he saw such potential but after discussing the piece more in-depth, I saw it too and decided to take his advice. I went back over it with just a few strokes, and I signed it. But how could this be? How could I have painted a four-foot by five-foot painting in five minutes and it would be one of my best? There was little labor, pain, lost sleep, and no major breakups or divorce. I just painted what I felt without fear, and it was brilliant!

This painting later received one of my favorite compliments. At one of my art shows, a man came by and said, "I just got back from the Chicago Art Museum, and I didn't see one piece that moved me as much as this one!"

So, here are my thoughts on overworking things: when I must paint quickly, my head doesn't have time to argue with my gut. It's the first draft and it's the best one because I'm tapping straight into my skill and don't have time for my head to get in the way. It doesn't matter if I do it in five minutes or two hours, but my best paintings tend to be the ones that I don't have time to overthink.

The other tendency—and women are especially susceptible to it—is to believe that if it's good, it can always be better. I don't know what it is about our sex that is driven by the need for improvement, but women tend to fine-tune or improve things when it would be better to leave well enough alone. That little extra tweak or final touch can sometimes ruin the whole piece. It shifts the dynamic of the painting and causes you to fix more and more things. Then you've lost your way and you can't find your way back.

We should learn from our male counterparts on this one. They tend to think, "If it's good, leave it alone."

Sometimes the sweet spots come fairly early in the painting process, and you don't believe that the painting could be done because you haven't really sweated or worked on it enough.

After we returned from the Dominican, Alex and I should have stepped back and assessed the relationship. It was clear we wanted different things. Our values weren't aligned. I should have taken my own advice and dropped the paintbrush and walked away from the painting. Then, our relationship would have been a sweet treasury of good memories.

Instead, I soldiered on. We worked on getting more time with his daughter. We hosted his brother for six months who was moving to the Pacific Northwest after a divorce from his wife in Alaska. Our families were bonding, and *my home* was becoming more and more *our home.*

The years slipped by and we made several more trips to the Dominican Republic—helping my son, Caleb, to launch his non-profit to bring used baseball gear and equipment to the kids in Alex's village, bringing medicine and art supplies, and volunteering to teach art at the local elementary school. The community knew me as *la esposa de Gaso,* referring to Alex by one of his nicknames and to me as his wife. They welcomed my family and me with open arms.

It became a tradition that Alex would leave for the Dominican Republic to be there with his family for Christmas and then I would join him in January. It was very important to him to connect with his family and especially during Christmas, and I supported him in that. But I longed for the deeper commitment of marriage, and I was becoming more restless with the way things were going. Living together was supposed to be temporary to test the waters before committing, but it was never my intention to stay that way.

The harder I tried, the more distant he became, and I was sensing that old familiar pattern, that same feeling I had with my ex-husband right before everything exploded. Had I overworked this relationship? Should I have taken my brushes and walked away years ago? I reminded myself that Alex was different, right? He was the guy with the beer hanging out on the sidelines, so he would never do anything to hurt me. He knew my past and he knew how long it took for me to open my heart again. He was so different from my ex-husband. Or was he?

Chapter 16:

Desperate? Throw Your Canvas in the Shower

One day, my student Lisa walked into Art-Women-Wine class and declared, "Well, I saved my painting by throwing it into the shower!"

I was shocked. Not so much at the method, but because she had found one, I hadn't tried. I've stuck sand, dirt, twigs, and other found objects onto my paintings before. I've painted over sections of the piece and begun again. I've blotted out portions completely. The idea of completely washing away a painting, however, was a new concept. She told us how she'd completed a beautiful abstract, but she'd failed to drop the paintbrush when she should have. She overworked it, layering over the top until it was terrible and completely ruined. In desperation, she threw it in the shower and scrubbed away at it with a scrub brush.

She continued, "I didn't have anything to lose because I absolutely hated the piece that was in front of me, so even if I ruined it, it couldn't be worse than what I had already done."

As the layers peeled off, the gist of a happy surprise emerged. We all gathered around and, sure enough, we could see those beautiful layers underneath with some patches of the new painting in sections over the top. The combination of the old and new was striking, and she was right: she certainly saved the piece by basically destroying it. Now, on occasion, all Art-Women-Wine members try the "Lisa technique" by throwing our paintings into the shower.

Have you ever started cooking a dish that wasn't working out well, but you just kept adding things until you end up with a bigger, wasted meal? I've dealt with Father Gio on this repeatedly. He'll be cooking something for one of our Italian art classes and will start with a sauce. Usually, he adds too much of one thing or another. Then, he has me run to Safeway for ingredients to balance it. By the end of the evening, we'll have spent three times the time and money to salvage what ends up being a terrible sauce. Sometimes it's better to cut your losses sooner. Recognize it's bad before botching it bigger later. If you're not willing to call it a failure when it is, you could end up with gallon-sized bags full of mediocre sauce that will eventually find their way into the garbage disposal.

When mixing paint, it's not uncommon to get a color you don't like but you keep painting with it because you think it will miraculously transform from your palette into something fabulous on your canvas. You think, *I don't want to waste this paint.* Instead, you'll hopefully get to a place where you can call it what it is—*wrong, off, bad, terrible, not worth saving, useless*—so you can get on the right path toward something beautiful as fast as you can.

"I didn't have anything to lose because I absolutely hated the piece in front of me. Even if I ruined it, it couldn't be worse than what I had already done."

It had been eight years trying to make a relationship work with Alex. I was a white, middle-class woman from the rural American west trying to make something last with a black, ex-professional baseball player from a rural part of the Dominican Republic. We had some things in common, like divorce, which only added to our difficulties of being together. Otherwise, the differences were vast.

I grew up in a stable family, on acreage, with horses and enough money for all our needs and many of our wants. Alex grew up in a big family in a little house—usually without running water and electricity—with his father being absent most of his life due to a long stint in the hospital. When I was sixteen, I was a popular girl in high school, driving my friends around in my car. When Alex was eighteen, he signed his baseball contract with a professional baseball team as a ticket out of poverty.

I had American views about money—I wanted to plan, to save, to be secure. He had island views about money—enjoy it all now because who knows what will happen tomorrow? I had parents who believed that they should provide for their children. He had parents who believed their children should provide for them. I parented my kids with a lot of interaction and oversight. He saw his daughter a couple of times a year and for a few weeks in the summer. I had a college education. He didn't finish high school. I spoke English and a little Spanish. He spoke Spanish and some English.

In a desperate attempt, we tried counseling. One counselor said we were completely incompatible. Another counselor worked with us and helped to improve certain aspects of our relationship, but it felt like we were trying to build a house without the right tools. As I look back, the signs were all there that the foundation was shaky. We cobbled together our relationship-house, patching up the leaks and breaks along the way. But it was a house of cards—one jolt and it could all come down.

The more effort I put in, the more I wanted it to succeed. It was excruciating to think that all that time and work wouldn't deliver what I wanted—a good marriage. Not just a ring and wedding, but a true marriage—a melding of goals, values, and beliefs. A unity of two hearts merged as one.

It was time to throw it in the shower and see if something good would come of it. Alex bought tickets to the Dominican Republic without letting me know. This was after he promised we would do Christmas and

New Year's Eve together for a change. He didn't even ask me if I'd join him later like we usually did. Instead, he was just informing me of his holiday plans, and they didn't include me. On December 15th, he left.

As I drove him to the airport, I felt in my gut that something was wrong. It all felt so strange—he was just a stranger sitting in my car. I dropped him off, a huge lump in my throat, and watched as he hustled to catch his flight.

Earlier in the fall, my son Weston said, "The guy lying on the couch, who is grumpy all the time and complaining— that's not the guy you fell in love with. Mom, I hate to see you give everything and he gives you nothing. It's your life. I want you to be happy, but I also want you to recognize that he's not the same and you deserve someone who gives as much as you do."

That conversation sat in the back of my mind. He was right. It seemed that over the years, Alex had become very complacent in our relationship. Why would he change or why would he marry me when he had all the benefits of marriage without having to commit? I hoped that when he returned, we could restart and try to find where we went wrong, or how we could save this.

I prayed; I cried. Then, I fasted for five days. I asked for the next steps, and to be specific, about what to do in this relationship. Something had shifted but I couldn't put my finger on it. Finally, the answer came to me. I knew that I needed physical distance from him. That was easy now but what about when he returned? I decided that we would not sleep together until we were married. Some people might say it was manipulative or too extreme. For me, however, it was my only hope to get some perspective because I knew that if we were intimate, I wouldn't be able to see clearly.

I showed him his new space when he arrived home and he tried to pull me close. His smell, his lips, and that beautiful smile had always overwhelmed me, but I held firm. He wasn't prepared for my strength and commitment to myself. There was a time limit too. I wasn't interested in being housemates. He would have a few months of living in the apartment which gave him ample time to look for another place to live or to make the decision for marriage. After eight years, if he was still not sure, then that would be the sign to move on.

In mid-February, I went away to Walla Walla with some friends. We stayed at a winery and wine-tasted throughout the area for the weekend. Alex. was invited but he declined. This was not a huge surprise; he had been distancing himself for a while now. Leaving family gatherings early, playing pool until 3 am, and being too exhausted to spend time with me had become his new normal. So, I went anyway and roomed with one of my besties, Elizabeth.

On our second day, I rolled over in bed as the sun was shining through this beautiful cottage window. I was half awake, skimming through messages when I saw a new WhatsApp message from a woman I didn't recognize but could see she was from the Dominican Republic. Maybe it was one of the moms of students I had taught down there or maybe it was another relative of Alex? I clicked it open and felt my heart drop into my stomach. I swallowed hard, as I google translated to clarify the message.

"Excuse me, Miss. I know that you don't know me, but I was Gaso's (Alex's) wife here in the Dominican Republic. He cheated on me with this woman (insert the woman's picture) and there were others."

I stopped breathing. *This couldn't be true. No way!* Then, like puzzle pieces falling into place, the overall picture emerged. The anger, the distance, and the solo vacations to the Dominican Republic, along with other clues that I had ignored, all passed through my mind and told the story. *Lord, I know I asked for next steps, but I didn't see this coming,* I prayed.

I think discovering infidelity is a lot like walking around a corner and being hit with a two-by-four. You lay there for a while trying to regain consciousness. It may be a long time before you can evaluate what really happened. The good news is that you won't die. I reminded myself that, on two other occasions, I had been cheated on and I survived it. I had been here before; it wasn't my first rodeo.

When I first find out about infidelity, the first thing I do is research. I find out everything I can. I reached out to the one family member I knew I could trust, and she confirmed my findings. He had every reason to lie, but my source who confirmed the stories had no reason to lie. She had also endured a divorce due to her husband's infidelity. She chose to tell the truth, and well—feminine loyalty—over family ties. Upon my return, Alex had already been tipped off that I knew something about him. I was calm, almost robotic, when I asked to see his phone. He knew he was caught, and he tried desperately to distract me. Liars are only liars if they are good at it, if it pays off, and he rivals my ex-husband in this regard. And he was still able to make me think, make me pause, and wonder ... was he speaking the truth? Then, I had to look at the evidence and away from what I wanted to be true. When the evidence was confirmed, I let Alex know that our relationship was over. I asked Alex to gather all his stuff and move out and stopped all contact with him.

The only way to get over grief is to move through it. I lost twenty pounds and not in a good way. Again, a giant spoon was scraping my guts out from just below my rib cage and I was becoming an empty shell. I was devastated. Plan C was an absolute disaster. The new dreams and hopes of a future together were shattered. I knew in my heart that I had given everything and yet, he still chose to cheat. I also had to grieve the betrayal of his whole family and community in the Dominican Republic because they all knew about it. I wrote a letter to all of them explaining how deeply I was hurt by each one; then I put it in my file box and never sent it. And what about his daughter? Would I be able to still see her? Sometimes, the grief seemed too great to overcome. How would I ever get over this massive loss?

My heart was in the shower, washing away the layers from the past eight years. Would there be anything worth salvaging when the deluge was done?

Chapter 17:

Put Your Painting in Time Out

Bailee walked in with a fresh new canvas. She is known in Art-Women-Wine class as "the girl who likes to paint *big*" and she is usually lugging a canvas double her size. But today I noticed that she didn't bring in the four-foot by four-foot boat painting she was working on and instead brought in a smaller canvas, tightly wrapped in cellophane.

Another Art-Women-Wine student, Michelle, slid over to her on her roller chair—a stool like the ones that the doctors sit on. Michelle claims she is the assistant teacher but like Michael Scott to Dwight Schrute in *The Office,* I always say, "assistant *to the* teacher," but it doesn't faze her. She wheels her authority and wisdom around, literally, with confidence and the whole class has been asking her for advice when I am busy.

Michelle said, "Good morning, Sunshine! What happened to your boats?" She eagerly followed up with, "Did you finish them already like the overachiever you are, doing extra homework this week?"

Bailee's eyes shifted as she began to unwrap the new canvas. "No, I wish," she replied. "Those stupid boats are sitting in the back of my closet in time-out! I'm so frustrated with them that I thought I'd just do something easy to give my mind a break."

Michelle slid back around to her canvas, waving her hands in the air and nodding her head in agreement. "I totally hear you. I have a few of those still sitting against the wall in my spare room—for years."

I walked over to talk a little more with Bailee now that my assistant-*to-the*-teacher had moved on. We chatted for a few minutes about the new piece she would start. Then, I assured her that it was perfectly okay to leave that painting in time-out for a while and when she was ready to pull it back out, I'd be there to help her finish it.

I have a painting that's been in time-out for

twenty years. Every time I pull it out to make changes, I get frustrated and send it back into time-out. I lean it so that it faces the wall in my studio closet. Originally, there were two of them in time-out, but I was able to finally finish the other one. And it sold. The finished piece has clouds I painted twenty years ago and clouds I painted just before it sold. My new style is less constrained, and the strokes seem freer and more relaxed. The juxtaposition of the old and new adds interest and texture.

My point is that this piece needed a twenty-year time-out. It took that long for my style to develop so I could finish it. When I began painting, I tried too hard, detailing each cloud, shadow, and highlight. I was tight, focusing until my eyes watered.

Eventually, I met another artist at a show, and I noticed that his clouds were breathtaking. I asked his advice about his process, and he shared his secret: take a picture with my camera lens out of focus or study the clouds with my glasses off. This helps me to see the blocks of lights and darks and deemphasizes the details. Brilliant! That tip was what I needed to change up my style of painting and I have been a "queen of clouds" ever since.

Once, I was painting with Grandma Dottie. We had worked on a painting together and she felt like thepiece was done, but she wasn't ready to sign it. She set the painting up on the mantel in her living room so we could see it. Then, she kicked back in her recliner next to my grandpa as they watched the news, and I dozed off on the couch behind them. Suddenly, I heard the recliner snap shut as Grandma exclaimed, "I've got it! I know what it needs. Come on, Elida, let's finish this painting!" She pulled the painting off the mantel, and we marched back into the studio so she could add the final touches. She was able to sign it that night.

I still don't really know what she saw or thought of in that time-out, but it was the break that gave her mind enough space to come up with a solution. So many times, I keep pushing through things. It's late and I keep going further and longer than I should. After all that wrestling, I'm angry and finally fall into bed frustrated. When I wake up the next day, I feel better. And when I walk into the room where the painting is, I'm pleasantly surprised that it's not as bad as I thought the night before. In fact, I realize that it's not really the painting that needs the time-out—it's me.

When I was angry with my parents, my

mom always quoted the scripture from Ephesians 4:26: "Don't let the sun go down on your anger." She implied that we shouldn't leave fights unresolved but should figure out a solution before going to bed. Now that I'm a little older, I dare to disagree with my devoted mother about that interpretation. I think the scripture isn't talking about solutions or resolutions but about holding grudges, getting bitter, or manipulating with the silent treatment. So many fights have become bigger because I'm tired or irrational, and what I really need is to go to bed. For me, the solution *is* sleep.

Remember that snarky email you sent to your boss, friend, sister, or whomever? Yeah, the one when you turned into an eighth grader and even resorted to name-calling. Don't you wish you had taken a time-out before sending it? Or that moment when you lost control and yelled at your kids while letting a few cuss words fly? Do you think a time-out might have helped?

I have big, deep feelings, which is really a way of saying that my relationships are going to see and hear about them. When I get fixated on something and I can't resolve it, my emotions become extreme. I cry. I shout. I say mean things. My emotions take the driver's seat, and reason and logic are shoved to the backseat. As I'm exploding, whoever is on the other end doesn't really have time to think. The result is a mess. Not only did I not accomplish anything, but I've also caused damage. In the morning, I have to say *I'm sorry.* And "sorry" can't undo the hurt I've caused.

I finally recognized that being sorry is sincere only if I make changes in my life to ensure that it doesn't happen again. In the past few years, I declared that I will no longer send heated text messages or emails to anyone late at night (and I like to work late at night). When emotions well up inside me, I write them all down *on paper* and let them sit awhile. Then, at a neutral time, when I am both rested and reasonable, I decide whether it's worth talking about.

Time-out is an effective strategy for your relationships and your work. The next time you feel frustrated with your painting, or you recognize that you've been triggered, it's time for a time-out. You'll have a clear perspective after some rest, whether it's about your life or your creative endeavor.

Bailee eventually brought back her boats and finished them. During their time-out, she identified new techniques and ideas that she hadn't thought of before. The time away from working on them allowed her to relax and come up with the solution to finish strong. The result was a beautiful painting that she proudly displayed.

My point is that the painting needed a twenty-year time-out. It took that long for my style to develop so I could finish it.

I was still in disbelief that Alex wasn't who I thought he was. Although his personality was very different from my ex-husband, his character was the same. I had been bamboozled again.

I realized I needed a time-out from the dating world. There was some soul searching that had to happen to discover why I consistently chose men who manipulate me and cheat on me. I was done running this pattern.

So, I put myself on a dating freeze for a year. My next step would focus on healing my heart. If I could also "fix my picker," all the better. I remembered that my friend, Donald Miller, had gone to a therapy retreat in Nashville a few years prior.

Donald even included the experience in his memoir *Scary Close*. He claimed it was life changing. That's what I needed: life changing.

I called Don and left him a long voice mail: "Hey there, Mister! It's your favorite señorita from the Pacific Northwest. Can you please tell me the name of that therapy camp you went to?" Then I launched into my current situation with my usual run-on sentences and too many details.

Don shot me back a short text: "Felipe, (my nickname my brother-in-law and he came up with) it sounds like "therapy camp" is exactly what you need. The name of the place is called Onsite and Betsy and I are happy to host you at our house for a few days prior to camp if you need a little R & R."

Don and Betsy had built a beautiful home on a large piece of land just outside of Nashville proper, including a "carriage house" where they host events and parties. Spending time there with two of the most genuine and giving people I know sounded like an oasis in the wilderness which was my life.

I took the Onsite Placement Test to see which workshop was best for me and then bought tickets to Nashville. This was just a few months after the breakup. Doing deep work on yourself can be so exhausting. This was not going to be easy and certainly not fun, but it was time. I realized that if I wanted to be free from this pattern and these relationships, I needed to clean out the closet of my childhood traumas.

Chapter 18:

Be Vulnerable, Always

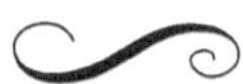

I had just arrived. Grandma Dottie met me at the door, hugged me, and, after I gave a quick wave to Grandpa, guided me quickly through the house and into her art studio.

"Look at all of this stuff I've collected," she squealed as she pulled out scraps of leather, pieces of broken stained glass, beads, and other collectibles. We scattered her treasures on the art table like a couple of magpies and started talking shop about what she could paint. I pulled out a few *National Geographic* magazines from her shelf for inspiration. As we rifled through the pages, she came upon an image of a volcano and in the foreground was a bald woman holding her head in pain. There were jagged lines across the woman's head that looked like cracks. She was drawn to this image and excitedly ripped it out of the magazine. We started putting the pieces together on the canvas—the woman with her head in pain was in the center and the glass pieces were placed around her. We added different mixed media pieces like a leather piece that looked like an eagle's face and a mountain exploding with lava pouring out of it.

Grandma wasn't really thinking. She was feeling and moving, and it was the canvas directing. As the painting came together, she finished it by pinning a gold pendant to the ear of the lady in pain as an earring.

She said, "This is what makes her human. Her beautiful earring makes her look less alien and reminds us of her femininity." She stepped back to take in the painting in its entirety. When I glanced over, I saw her tears. She exclaimed, "She's me. That's me in the painting. That's how I feel."

My heart sank. She had spent the last forty years of her life battling cancer intermittently. She fought bravely, but the cancer was back and with a vengeance. My grandmother was in pain. She was so vibrant and joyful that she helped me to forget her pain. She was so focused on living that she helped me forget she was dying. In the end, she taught me about both.

She wiped away her tears and headed into the other room to bring Grandpa in to see it. I was worried that he'd dismiss her efforts as "cotchy-botchy," a slang term he used for junk art—which is what he usually called any of our mixed media paintings. Thankfully, he responded differently this time. He was impressed and told her so. He said that he could feel that the painting came from somewhere deep inside her.

Next, Grandma wanted to share her painting with my aunt and cousin who lived next door. She started toward the door and then hesitated. "What if they think this piece is scary-looking or stupid?" she asked.

"Grandma," I said, "I watched you create this piece from your heart. You put pieces in it that spoke to you, and you didn't think about how it would be received. You just created with feeling and passion. No matter what they think, it doesn't matter because, for you, this was a healing piece and it's important that you are happy with it."

She took a deep breath and gave me a soft smile as she hugged me around my shoulders and squeezed me tight. Then we walked across the yard to my aunt's house and knocked on the door. Grandma lifted the piece for them to see. Her face betrayed her need for acceptance.

Aunt Debbie and my cousin, Ehren, both looked at the painting for a long time. Finally, Aunt Debbie said, “Mom, this is good. I can feel your pain in this painting. It’s a very strong piece.” Grandma’s smile brightened and the tension broke. Excitedly, she began explaining the different parts in it.

It was a special time for me. I was able to witness Grandma’s shift from creating for the world to creating from her heart. She reminded me how to silence the noise of what (we think) people want and listen to the canvas. Our creations are so much stronger when we share what’s really happening. This is how powerful pieces are made—when artists paint from their raw emotions and thoughts. They push away outside influences and find an inner voice.

I remember the first night I painted after I split with my ex-husband. A bottle of wine and a lot of anger went into that piece. I chose a big canvas and I let everything go onto it. I didn’t hold back to make it pretty. I didn’t soften the edges. I just painted exactly how I was feeling at that time. When some of my friends and fans first saw this piece, they didn’t recognize it as mine since it wasn’t my palette of color or my typical style. Still, everyone was drawn to it. The unguarded and open emotions resonated.

When you are trying to please others or force the canvas into submission, it will turn out flat. Something will be missing. But when you come to the canvas with an open mind and heart, you'll find that you enjoy the process of painting so much more. In the end, your piece will be authentic and impactful. Not everyone will love what you do but they can at least say that they feel something when they see it.

I was able to witness Grandma's shift from creating for the world to creating from her heart.

I arrived in Nashville on a balmy weekday afternoon. Don, Betsy and their new baby girl, Emmaline, were all there to greet me. With a quick tour of the house and a beautiful dinner on their southern-style wraparound porch, I could already feel my anxiety start to calm down. Then, there were a few lazy days by their pool and me reading and drinking all their seltzer water.

Did I really need to go to this therapy workshop? My personality seeks to avoid down and depressing times as much as possible. This special room at Don and Betsy's seemed to be made for me and—I wouldn't be much trouble. I would replace the seltzers, eventually, and I am a master at making Swedish hotcakes. Plus, when Emmaline got a little bigger, maybe she wanted private paint classes? I'm just upstairs, honey!

Donald reminded me of the reason I was there and reluctantly I packed my bags and he drove me out to the compound. Onsite is nestled in a little town about an hour outside of Nashville. It turned out therapy camp wouldn't be physically uncomfortable. Their camp cabins were actual houses with wood floors and marble bathroom vanities and each room had individual queen beds with fluffed feather pillows and beautiful linens. This was certainly my style of camping. The food was also top notch—fresh salmon, steak, and other delicious entrees. The first night, I grabbed my little cafeteria tray, gathered my food, and bellied up to the table next to a few single girls who looked like they hadn't established a group yet. "Hi, I'm Elida and nice to meet ya!" Introductions were made around the table as we all settled in.

We had to turn in our phones, and we were not allowed to share what we did for a living. It seemed like a strange request, but later I learned that sometimes celebrities would join, and the moment people figured out who they were, everyone would start treating them differently. We were thirty-three people from all over the world, with different careers and backgrounds, but we were all stuck together for one reason: we needed help, and we needed healing. Every day we would have group therapy sessions together and then break into smaller groups in different buildings. There was no alcohol or smoking allowed. For some, this was a major challenge.

I was in a small group with eight other women. As everyone was jockeying for some sort of position in the group, I looked around and wondered, "What's this person's story and why is she here?" Of course, like every other person there, I believed everyone else's story and issues were way worse than my own. Over the course of that week, I worked hand and hand with each of these women as we shared our own struggles and traumas. Some of us were survivors of sexual abuse, abusive spouses, or toxic relationships. It was as if we all had these childhood traumas that we had sealed in mason jars and shoved them back deep into our emotional pantries. None of us wanted to deal with it. Since those traumas hadn't been sealed properly, they had spoiled and bubbled over, making a huge mess. Cleaning is always more fun with friends and this emotional cleaning was no exception. We cried, we shared, we laughed, and we cried again. I saw some serious breakthroughs and had some "aha" moments as I pulled out all the hurts from my childhood to present. In just one week, we had all changed.

At the end of the session, we were all sitting around the campfire, roasting marshmallows and singing camp songs. Our phones were returned to us. Secretly I dreaded getting mine back because this was sacred, healing, and safe. My phone meant responsibilities and work and I wasn't ready to face the outside world again. The laughs continued and more stories were shared. Everyone was excited to take a few pictures of all our new friends. It was a magical night but the dread of going back to the real world was palpable. I may never see these people again and yet they know more about my life than some of my closest friends and family. The next day, I gathered up my stuff as I headed back to Don and Betsy's house before flying to Portland. It was a good idea to have a few more days of pool lounging because I knew that when I got home, I would need to confront some people and patterns in my pursuit of healing.

That spring, I confronted my parents for the way that they had handled my sexual abuse. I was five years old when the babysitter decided to "play mommy and daddy." I don't remember how long the abuse happened, but I had hid that inside, burying it for years until my stomach aches became so bad that my parents took me to the doctor. The doctor told them it was stress. But how could I be stressed? They raised me on this beautiful farm out in the country in the most idyllic setting you could imagine. Finally, when I was twelve, the stomach aches were still present, and I told my parents the secret I had been holding. They were so sad about what happened but then they were paralyzed as to what to do. By this time, that babysitter was in college and wasn't going to be babysitting me anymore. They thought the problem was over, so let's just move on. Their lack of action or follow-through conveyed this message to me: *You aren't important enough to protect.*

I know this wasn't their intention but when you are a kid and you reach out to your parents about something horrendous that happened to you and they do nothing, that message can come across. Then, I internalized it deep into my soul. It became part of my identity. This message stayed with me as I went through different relationships. It rattled my self-esteem. I felt that I wasn't enough nor was I valuable enough to be protected. Even though the abuse was over forty years ago, it still haunted me.

Something I really learned at Onsite was that those core beliefs we adopt as children play out in our adult relationships. It made sense, but how do you fix it? Then there was other abuse that happened within our family with some of my extended relatives and yet the family still allowed the perpetrator to continue to come to our family functions where kids were present. Why wasn't anyone standing up? Why were these poor girls subject to seeing him and being around him if they wanted to be involved in this family function? Plus, why were we all sitting back and allowing him access to the next batch of girls? After Onsite, a fire was lit in my soul. I sent a letter to all of our family members to warn them of this person and asked that our family would stand up for these girls who were victims of sexual abuse. I also shared my stance that I would no longer be involved in any more family functions if this perpetrator continued to be there and have free access to our kids. I stood in solidarity with the victims. The ripple effect was huge. Some agreed with me, some called me names, and some didn't say anything. I was surprised at who stood up with me and who just ignored my warning and dismissed my concerns.

I worked extremely hard in getting them to understand that sexual abuse must be reported, and we must stand up and do our part in protecting the innocent. In the end, more girls came to me and shared their stories and because I was so vulnerable in sharing about my own abuse, they felt brave enough to stand up in their situations as well.

That summer, I called the police station and reported my sexual abuse from when I was five years old. I also reported what I knew about the perpetrator in our extended family and encouraged each of his victims to report as well. It didn't matter how long ago the abuse happened because that wound could never heal until I faced it. For me, as uncomfortable and hard as it was to report, something inside me lifted when I shared my story with the police officer. It was the completion of a cycle that had been left open and a lie I had adopted my whole life. I was doing for myself what my parents didn't do for me.

I found an old picture of "little Elida" when I was about three years old. I have her looking at me from my dresser and I'm reminded each day that my job is to take care of her. I am so proud of how I handled my situation now and that I led with vulnerability and love. I know that by standing up, I encouraged others to do the same. If you are reading this right now and you have endured sexual abuse of any kind and it was never handled correctly, I want to encourage you to pick up the phone, call your local police station and make a report. It doesn't matter if it was a long time ago or how long the statute of limitations is. What matters is that you do the right thing by reporting it. You will feel better, lighter, and can start truly healing. Be brave. Be vulnerable always. I am with you, standing right next to you, holding your hand and cheering you on!

Chapter 19:

All Paintings Go Through Puberty

The room was filled with artists quietly painting beautiful colors over their canvases. The atmosphere was calm and happy—many students were sipping wine between strokes. I raised my voice to get the attention of the group: "Okay, everyone, scoop up a few skin tone colors with your palette knife. We're starting with the face, and then we'll add the arms, hands, and legs."

I looked around to see that people were following directions. Right away, I noticed that Mandy just sat there, her eyes downcast. I walked over to her table, leaned down beside her, and whispered, "Hey, are you okay?"

She glanced over at me and gave an apologetic smile. "I really love my background and I'm scared to put all of this paint over it and ruin everything," she said. I stood up and scanned the room and realized that Mandy wasn't the only one looking anxious.

I was going to have to wreck the mood. I clapped for attention. "All right, everyone, listen up. We are about to hit junior high. Things are going to get very ugly. Your painting is going into full-fledged puberty—braces, headgear, and acne. But I want to assure you that *all paintings must go through puberty*, just like people. To become beautiful masterpieces, they must have an ugly stage. So, are you ready?"

I went over to Mandy's canvas and started scraping up some of the skin tone colors with her palette knife and kept talking to her calmly as I began to put the paints on her canvas. It looked horrible—it always does—but with me sitting next to her and encouraging her along, she reluctantly took the palette knife and kept going. I got up to check on the rest of the class and heard the moans, groans, and complaints. I made several stops to coax them through, hoping they'd trust me long enough to experience what was next.

Once they'd made a mess on the canvases, they loosened up and stopped trying to control their paintings so much. It allowed for some real innovative genius to show up. The next step was to clean up a few lines with their angled brushes and, when they did this, everything came together.

Mandy was the first to exclaim, "Whoo-hoo! I made it through middle school!" Many of the other students were smiling as they saw their paintings rounding the corner to adulthood. In the end, we all stood outside the winery holding our paintings proudly.

It doesn't matter how long you've been painting or how good you are, there is usually a stage of the process where the piece is ugly. I say, "It has to look bad before it looks good!" When students get the most frustrated, I remind them that their painting must go through puberty. Nobody wants to go back to seventh grade and deal with body odor, body changes, insecurity, or awkward school dances. But we all had to go through it to grow up. Art must go through a similar process.

That's not to say that the process is easy. Sometimes my painting just flows out, but even then, there is a moment when the painting doesn't look good. Other times, I fight and wrestle with the painting for much longer, sometimes years. The crux is usually about halfway through the process, after the dark layers. When you begin to put in the lighter and brighter tones, the piece starts to come together. Sometimes we want to jump ahead to all the bright colors and not create depth with deeper tones, but if we do we miss powerful steps in the process and lessen the beauty of the piece.

I just painted a holiday llama that looks like a bad mix between Smeagol from *Lord of the Rings* and a bad Santa. I'm calling him "Smeagol Santa," and he's so ugly and terrible that I just want to burn that painting up. It hit puberty so hard. It's embarrassing that a professional artist could make something so ugly. I've continued to work on it and started another one that turned into a bear-bunny. I'm not laughing but everyone else is. Again, not what I was going for, but both paintings are just hanging out in seventh grade right now.

But I have enough experience to know that you shouldn't try to rush through puberty, covering all that acne up with makeup. Everyone can see that it's not ready yet. Give those pieces some space and time. Don't put them front and center and under the spotlight; they're embarrassed by how they look. Instead, tuck them away for a few days or for however long it takes. Eventually, you'll come back to it when it's ready to step into maturity.

I know this because I have spent hours and hours feeling frustrated and angry at a piece, only to feel elated and happy when I give it a few days and a fresh look. Learning how to deal with the puberty stage is important. All of us have gone through it, and—though we sometimes need to be reminded—it never lasts forever.

When students get the most frustrated, I remind them that their painting must go through puberty. Nobody wants to go back to seventh grade and deal with body odor, body changes, insecurity, or awkward school dances. But we all had to go through it to grow up. Art must go through a similar process.

Facing my sexual abuse and forcing the people who were around at the time to deal with it was ugly. I ruffled a lot of feathers, and the fallout made a mess. I did it anyway because I knew the only way to put it behind me was to go through this. We would be a healthier and stronger family once we stood up for what was right.

Sometimes when you stand up, people must face their own past as well. I was coming to the end of my year-long freeze from dating. I was getting pretty good at saying no to any dates offered or any male friendship for that matter. Once I was out dancing and I got chatting with this Chileno guy who had a great smile and the cutest dimples. He asked for my number so we could connect again outside of dancing. That sounds like a date, so I informed him, "I'm not dating right now."

"It's not a date," he argued. "I just want to meet as friends."

I asked, "Do you have a penis?"

His eyes widened and he nodded his head to say yes.

"Well, if you have a penis, we can't be friends. My counselor told me I can't even be friends with any guys right now!" We did end up becoming friends and to this day he teases me about asking him that.

With some encouragement from friends and family, I reluctantly put myself out there again. I had never done dating apps before, so reluctantly I made a profile on an app that seemed a little more conservative. You only got a few matches each day, but it was kind of fun to see who the algorithm thought might interest me. I talked with a few and started to get a little more comfortable in this strange new way of dating. One guy and I were chatting for a bit and suddenly, he disappeared. I checked back on the conversation, tried to see our history and "poof" he was gone. I thought he had an Instagram and went into FBI mode. Aha! I found him. I was so excited and shot him a quick note, "Hey, so glad I found you. I'm new at the dating app thing and there must be a glitch or something in that stupid app because we were talking and then you disappeared."

The chirp, chirp, chirp of crickets answered me. That was weird. I mean we were having such a great conversation and I thought he would be thrilled that our connection wasn't lost. Maybe something happened? Maybe he was hit by a train or abducted by aliens? Maybe his phone was stolen or his identity swiped? I needed help with this dating app thing in the modern world, so I decided to ask my son, Caleb. In college, he had been in the dating scene for a while now.

He was home from college and getting a glass of water when I started to tell him about my dilemma. He raised his eyebrows to let me know he was listening.

"Well, I was on this app and chatting with this guy and all of a sudden he disappeared!"

Caleb gave me a little nod, still drinking.

"So I thought something must be really wrong with this app and started to look for him on social media."

Caleb's forehead wrinkled.

I continued, "The good news is, I found him on Instagram and the bad news is he's not replying."

At this, Caleb spit out his drink and started laughing. Water was coming out of his nose, and he was crying and laughing so hard. In between water dripping from his mouth and tears rolling down his eyes, he choked out, "Mom, you were GHOSTED!"

"What is ghosted?" I asked.

He explained it to me and filled me in on how dating works in this decade.

I was flabbergasted and angry. "Who does that?" I asked. "Like when did we as a society decide that when you are done talking to someone, you just disappear. That's so rude!" I was ready to delete this stupid app and thought maybe it was a good idea if, instead of doing just a yearlong freeze, I would do a forever freeze and join Fr. Gio as a nun. I'm just not cut out for this dating business especially in this era. I put my app and my dating on pause so I could regroup.

Then I remembered that perhaps this was puberty for my dating life. It had to get ugly before it got beautiful. I couldn't demand that the entire world return to normalcy when people found other people organically at places of mutual interest or through mutual friends. The world had moved on. I had to deal with the acne of misunderstood chats, the body odor of bad dates, and the body changes from the pictures they posted to the reality sitting across the table. But I hoped that through it all I would eventually be able to eventually handle this new dating style with confidence and maturity.

But how long would the ugly stage last?

Chapter 20:

You Are an Artist. Yes, You

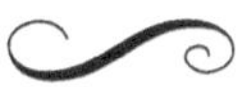

I expect all my students, from beginning level to experienced, to show their work at our annual city art show, but it took some convincing to get Marianne to show her artwork at the chiropractor clinic downtown. She was resistant to sharing her work with anyone. Marianne is a fifth-grade teacher, and she is also a talented photographer and painter. I'm pretty sure she can sew and play an instrument as well. She's one of those creative people who succeeds at whatever she wants to do, but she's unaware of just how brilliant she is.

The night went well. As I made my rounds to the artists' venues, I reminded them of the after-party at my studio. When I visited Marianne, I was pleased to see people giving her positive feedback about her work. Then I said, "Hey, Marianne! Just wanted to remind you that, after the show tonight, we are having an artist reception at the studio for the artists."

Marianne looked at me blankly. "Okay, so why are you telling me this?" she asked.

I laughed and said, "I'm telling you this because *you* are one of the artists and the reception is to celebrate *you*!"

The look of surprise and delight on her face was priceless! Even on the night of the event where she was showing her artwork, she still didn't see herself as a "real artist."

Sometimes, I feel a little like Marianne. Who am I to teach? I don't have a teaching degree. Who am I to write a book? I'm not a writer. It's that little voice, that nasty one, that says, "You are a fraud."

I know many self-taught artists who have become proficient by reading books, watching YouTube videos, and trial and error. And even though their work is shown in galleries, and they have collectors all over the world, they still feel like they aren't serious artists because they don't have any formal schooling.

A few years ago, I got a big grant to teach about fifty teachers how to teach art in schools. I was very excited about it and began carefully preparing for my presentation. Then, doubt crept in. I was going to teach to an auditorium full of teachers who held higher degrees, and in teaching no less, and yet I was expected to teach them. *Who am I to teach all these teachers? I don't even have a teaching degree. I'm just an artist!* I thought.

The morning of my panic attack, I shared my worries with a friend. He assured me that I was capable and that I was a professional. Even though I didn't have as much schooling as some of these teachers, I had years of teaching experience.

"Treat them like they are your students," he said, "because today, they are. They are not your peers or your superiors." I contemplated this and realized he was right. I shouldn't see them as teachers who were more educated. As far as my specialty, they weren't. Many of them feared art and feared teaching art to their students even more. I had been doing both of those things for years. I took a big breath and reminded myself that I could do this!

As I was driving to the school that morning, I remembered a story about Grandma Dottie. She went from being a high school secretary to being the director of a grant program for oceanography at the University of Southern California. She flew back from a huge conference consisting mostly of doctors where she was the keynote speaker. My grandfather picked her up from the airport. After greeting him, she got in the passenger seat and leaned back, exhausted. Then she said, "Wes, I don't know how long I can fake this. I'm way over my head!"

They were passing by the cityscape of Los Angeles and Grandpa asked, "Do you see the lights at the top of those skyscrapers?" She opened her eyes and looked up at them. He continued, "Those penthouses are full of CEOs who are 'just faking it!' Right now, you may not feel like an authority, but I know you, and in time, you will be the expert!"

If you are questioning your abilities or qualifications, remember you are not alone. Everyone has those uncertainties. The important thing is to show up and do what you know how to do. Trust that if you are asked to speak or if you are invited to teach or paint or whatever it is that you do, you will probably feel like you are just faking it, but in time, you will be the master.

Who am I to teach? I don't have a teaching degree. Who am I to write a book? I'm not a writer. It's that little voice, that nasty one, that says, "You are a fraud."

In this new chapter of my life, I realize that dating someone healthy just feels wrong. It's kind of like when I get somewhere early, I always feel like I must have forgotten something. I must be missing something because I'm always late and being early just feels weird. I feel uneasy, worried, and off.

Seriously, my next book may be titled, *I Don't Feel Good Unless I Feel Bad* because for so long, I have invited stressful relationships into my life. I had become used to feeling uncertain and uneasy that it felt normal. Apparently, I have a type, and that type is bad news.

With all that work I did at Onsite and the healing I've done in my life since then, I feel much more confident that I'll be wiser in my choosing. Somehow, I believed that being peaceful would be boring. You have to admit that chaos is dynamic, and it can be exciting! But I think it's time. My old patterns no longer serve me, and I can now say, "I used to do this, but now I choose this." Just like learning anything new, I know that it will take some time.

I've been trying to remind myself that I am healthy now. I have dealt with my past. I have faced my mistakes. I have challenged my assumptions. I have accepted my shortcomings. I am willing to take new paths. Truthfully, there is nothing holding me back ... but me.

Already, I've had some snafus. There was Mr. Gallery Director in the Chelsea District of New York City who had a million-dollar smile and a voice as smooth as silk, but he also had three babies with three different mammas and there were many more red flags. He was ready to fly me back to New York City to see him and I already was dreaming of a loft in the city. But when I looked at my picture of my little self and listened to that small voice that said, "Elida, this is so familiar and exciting, but you know it's not good for you." Then, there was the Cuban model in Mexico City. Mamma Mia! Was he ever beautiful and... dangerous. The invitation to Cancun sounded like so much fun, but the chaperone from the Mexican cartel helped me to decline. I knew where this was heading and if I wanted anything different, I knew it had to stop.

I fail; I do. The difference is that I recognize the pattern earlier and I can redirect quicker. That's progress. I think in time, as I keep practicing this new way of living, I won't even be attracted to those unhealthy people anymore. Before they make it onto my radar, I'll shut that energy down. I know it will take time, but I also believe that the more I walk in my purpose and stay in God's light, I will repel the darkness. Health attracts health.

It's taken me a lifetime to stop living out the lie that I am not enough. I am enough and I deserve to be loved fully and completely. It doesn't have to be chaotic, uncertain, and unsettling. I can rest in knowing that I can fully trust myself and God to show me the way. There is nothing that we can't handle. Together we can do all things. Just as Marianne is an artist, and my grandmother became a director, I am a healthy person learning what it means to be healthy. And you know what? It hasn't been boring at all!

Chapter 21:

Sign Your Painting

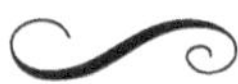

Carrie stepped back from her colorful palette angel painting and looked pensive. Then she asked, hopefully, "Am I done?"

I sat down beside her, put my hand on her shoulder, and said, "You know, if you aren't quite sure, give it a little time. You can set this up on the mantel and look at it for a while. See it in a different light. Get a fresh perspective. You might want to give it a little touch of something. If you want my truthful opinion, however, I think it's done or pretty darn close. When you are ready, trust your gut and *sign it*!"

Carrie nodded. I had the pen ready, and she took it from my hand. Then, she leaned down to the bottom right corner of her painting and wrote her name.

"Woooohoooo!" I shouted as I threw my hands in the air. "Attention everyone! I am pleased to announce that Carrie has finished her painting! Carrie, you know what to do." I extended my hand to guide her toward the bell hanging in my studio. She strode towards it and lifted it off its stand and started ringing. The entire studio was clapping and cheering, and I grabbed my phone to capture the moment.

This is one of the favorite parts of my job. There is such a sense of satisfaction to have labored at something and complete it. And while some people may be just about getting stuff done, I like to pause and celebrate. Take a moment to look around from the mountaintop and enjoy the view.

Whenever someone rings the bell, I am reminded of perhaps the most powerful lesson my Grandma Dottie taught me.

One day she called me,"Hi, Hon, it's Grandma. I just wanted to let you know that I flunked chemo."

I was silent for a moment, trying to process what she was saying. She had tried all sorts of treatments. This chemotherapy was the last resort and hope.

"What are you going to do?" I asked.

"Well, I've decided that I'm going to Portugal!" Then, she launched into all her fun plans and whom she would spend time with.

I listened, perplexed, as her attitude didn't match up with what I was hearing. When I hung up, I contemplated her decision and her frame of mind. Eventually, I realized that she had probably spent plenty of time thinking these results over. She had likely grieved it in private. And she wasn't ignoring reality. Instead, she was facing it and accepting it. She knew that her painting was almost finished. She was placing the masterpiece of her life on the mantel, and after a little splash of red (or a final trip to Portugal), she was ready to sign it with a flourish.

Grandma Dottie did go to Portugal. And Hawaii. She also had a massive party with the entire family. All the grandkids carried her like she was the Queen of Sheba on a chariot (her big wingback chair) out to the garden where we took some final family pictures and enjoyed our last moments with her.

While I stayed with her, she convinced me to paint her slingback canvas chairs. She wanted poppies painted on them and she was adamant that they be painted. She would have had me painting over her bedroom walls too if I had more time. She was asking me questions about pieces and projects as if she were going to live forever. She didn't stop living, not for one second.

Sure, she was probably afraid, but she was brave in how she handled it—spending joyful time with her friends and family, adding a little dash of color before signing her finished work. It was perhaps one of the most beautiful things I've ever witnessed.

I look back on the lessons I teach in art class and reflect on how they relate to my own life.

- My love isn't for everyone.
- Keep my supportive circle of Fab Five friends and family around me and rely on them as I make decisions.
- Be brave and bold, because there aren't many rewards for the weak-hearted.
- Most things I stress about aren't life and death situations.
- Go for an approximation of what I want rather than perfection.
- Stay positive.

- Remember that beginnings are probably going to be failures but that's the only way to success.
- I am meant for someone special, so don't fret when someone doesn't return my love.
- Sometimes, I'll have to let go of good people or good things in my life for the greater good of my overall life.
- I won't compare myself to others, though, because it kills my creativity and excitement for life.
- Be willing to do a poor imitation of the life I hope for until I get the hang of it.
- Layer it over with another experience if it turns out badly.
- Recognize that the tough times make the joyful times all the sweeter.
- It's important to know when to walk away, go for a reset, or give a situation a time-out.
- And after the time-out, being vulnerable and fearless, and maybe even a toss in the shower, you must accept that it's time to finish the painting.

In these instances, it's important to remember the joy I felt while creating as well as all the time I overcame frustration to give it my best. As I gaze over the gallery of my life, I try not to see all my experiences with judgments of "good" or "bad." Instead, I see them as complete. Each painting, relationship, or season was my very best at that time. I am proud of my progress as an artist and a human being.

As I reflect on my path and relationships, I've applied Grandma's lesson of how to sign my paintings and face the end of important phases of my life. I've signed the painting on my marriage, on my relationship with Sam and Alex. I've signed the painting of my past and forgiven the people who have hurt me. I've signed the painting on many little relationships that turned out to just be sloppy copies. And now, as I write this final chapter, I am solo again. Time will tell when that season of my life is finished.

So, sign your paintings. You may have made decisions that hurt someone and caused the relationship to end prematurely. Make amends, say you're sorry, and own your part (that's the little dash of red). And then sign it.

Signing it doesn't mean you approve or applaud what's on the canvas. I have some paintings in which my mistakes are glaring but I can't really fix them without altering its soul. It would make the painting a completely different piece. It's better to acknowledge them, learn from them, and do better on the next one.

Grandma Dottie taught me a lot about living, but she also taught me about dying and about how to finish well. She taught me how to bring a painting—and life—to a close, by giving it that final pop of red at the very end and then signing it with a flair.

As I gaze over the gallery of my life, I try not to see all my experiences with judgments of "good" or "bad." Instead, I see them as complete. Each painting, relationship, or season was my very best at that time. I am proud of my progress as an artist and a human being.

I have been working on three massive commission paintings for almost nine months now. Each piece of the triptych represents a different state and the places my patrons have lived during that time. On the left is Washington, in the center is California, and on the right is Colorado. In the background I have glued down maps, words, dates, pictures and important artifacts that are meaningful to them. In the front, I've painted important symbols, figures, and items that have personal significance. There is Roxy, their dog, jogging up the dirt road in the first painting and their cats are hidden in different parts of the other paintings.

I ask my Art-Women-Wine students, "What do you all think?"

"Well, I think you should move the Redwoods up and the wineries down below the Golden Gate Bridge," says Catherine.

"And you should hide the cats in the forest," pipes in Lisa. The opinions keep coming and I keep listening, changing the painting with every new voice. I have spent hours, days, and weeks painting over things and alternating between trusting myself and abandoning my gut feelings. It is the biggest series of work I've done in a long time. It must be perfect.

I am working late. I've lost track of time, but I'm in a good flow. The pieces are almost done. I can feel it. I add an orchid in the top left corner, the last of the details I know that my clients will love. They are her favorite and I love hiding things into pieces for my collectors to find later. I paint it into the background and highlight one of the petals. I take a big breath and back up to see all three pieces as one final set.

It's good. I know it's right and I know it's done. I let out a huge sigh of relief as I reflect on these past few years, all the things I've overcome, and who I am right now. I am Elida, an artist. I'm also Mom, Nonna (my grandson's name for me), businesswoman, author, salsa-dancing extraordinaire, and world traveler. I grab my gold pen and scribble my signature on the bottom right corner.

It's three o'clock in the morning and there is no one in the studio. No one to *oooh* and *ahhh* or even to criticize. No one to cheer me on or to clap their hands. Still, I walk to the other side of the studio. I close my eyes and imagine that Grandma is there and cheering alongside me. I can see her smiling and giving me a little wink of approval. Then, I grab the bell and start ringing.

Epilogue

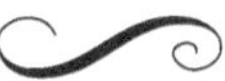

The paintings made it to my clients in Colorado. They sent me a video of them walking in their front door and seeing the pieces hung for the first time. "Elida, they are spectacular, even better than we imagined. They truly transform the space and the overall feeling of the house!" I've started to get used to feeling calm and rested. Something has shifted. Could this be my mid-life crisis? While most people take chances because they're used to playing it safe, I may be experiencing these changes in reverse order. Maybe it's just getting older and wiser. I feel settled and relaxed. I realize that I don't need to conquer anything and, in fact, I'm quite content with doing less.

Regarding relationships, there is a new special someone. I've already tried to fast-forward my life and figure out the end of the story, but I was reminded today by my counselor, "Stop getting in your own way and just be curious and present." I asked her for homework and she replied, "I think that's enough. It's a full time job being present!" So, I guess that's what I'll try to do—enjoy the process without trying to control the outcome.

I'm considering revamping the focus on my business. It may even be time to "sign the painting" on a few aspects of it. After all these years of teaching art, which have taught me so much, I'm looking to learn some new lessons.

Next year, I have a milestone birthday to celebrate—the big 5-0. And, of course, as you probably know by now, I live by the slogan,"Go big or go home!" So what do you think of my plan to celebrate by visiting fifty countries in my 50th year? I know it sounds crazy but, then again, it could be fun! I could start in Africa with an art safari in Tanzania or kick off the year in South America learning tango in Argentina.

Or maybe I should spend that year painting, cooking cinnamon rolls with my grandson and taking long walks in nature. What do you think?

www.ingramcontent.com/pod-product-compliance
Lightning Source LLC
LaVergne TN
LVHW100523110826
845146LV00002B/755

* 9 7 9 8 9 8 8 8 7 7 9 0 5 *